Army Regulation 601–270
OPNAVINST 1100.4C CH-1
MCO 1100.75F
COMDTINST M 1100.2E

Personnel Procurement

Military
Entrance
Processing
Station (MEPS)

Rapid Action Revision (RAR) Issue Date: 13 September 2011

Headquarters
Departments of the Army,
the Navy,
the Marine Corps, and
the Coast Guard
Washington, DC
23 March 2007

UNCLASSIFIED

SUMMARY of CHANGE

AR 601-270/OPNAVINST 1100.4C CH-1/MCO 1100.75F/COMDTINST M 1100.2E
Military Entrance Processing Station (MEPS)

This rapid action revision, dated 13 September 2011--

o Implements the Don't Ask, Don't Tell Repeal Act of 2010 by deleting all
  references to homosexual conduct, to separation for homosexual conduct, and
  to homosexual conduct being a bar to entry or induction into the Armed Forces
  (deleted para 9-21).

o Adds the word "forcible" (para E-4, bullet 34).

o Makes administrative changes (app A: corrected publication titles marked and
  obsolete forms marked; glossary: deleted unused acronyms and corrected
  titles/abbreviations as prescribed by Army Records Management and
  Declassification Agency).

Headquarters
Departments of the Army,
the Navy,
the Marine Corps, and
the Coast Guard
Washington, DC
23 March 2007

*Army Regulation 601–270
*OPNAVINST 1100.4C
CH–1
*MCO 1100.75F
*COMDTINST M 1100.2E

Personnel Procurement

Effective 4 April 2007

Military Entrance Processing Station (MEPS)

By Order of the Secretary of the Army, Navy, Marine Corps and Coast Guard:

RAYMOND T. ODIERNO
General, United States Army
Chief of Staff

Official:

JOYCE E. MORROW
Administrative Assistant to the
Secretary of the Army

MARK E. FERGUSON III
Vice Admiral, U.S. Navy
Deputy Chief of Naval Operations
(Manpower, Personnel, Training
and Education)

R.E. MILSTEAD, JR.
Lieutenant General, U.S. Marine Corps
Deputy Commandant for Manpower and
Reserve Affairs

RONALD T. HEWITT
Rear Admiral, U.S. Coast Guard
Assistant Commandant for Human Resources

History. This publication is a rapid action revision (RAR). This RAR is effective 20 September 2011. The portions affected by this RAR are listed in the summary of change.

Summary. This regulation covers military entrance processing station operational policies, programs, and procedures. It implements DOD Directive 1145.2 governing personnel enlisting in the military and the processing of Selective Service registrants.

Applicability. This regulation applies to the active Army, the Army National Guard/Army National Guard of the United States, the U.S. Army Reserve, the Navy, the Air Force, the Marine Corps, and the Coast Guard, unless otherwise stated. This regulation applies to all personnel who operate unit mail rooms at company and battalion levels. During mobilization, procedures in this publication can be modified to support policy changes as necessary.

Proponent and exception authority. The proponent of this regulation is the Deputy Chief of Staff, G–1. The proponent has the authority to approve exceptions or waivers to this regulation that are consistent with controlling law and regulations. The proponent may delegate this approval authority, in writing, to a division chief with the proponent agency or its direct reporting unit or field operating agency, in the grade of colonel or the civilian equivalent. Activities may request a waiver to this regulation by providing justification that includes a full analysis of the expected benefits and must include formal review by the activity's senior legal officer. All waiver requests will be endorsed by the commander or senior leader of the requesting activity and forwarded through their higher headquarters to the policy proponent. Refer to AR 25–30 for specific guidance.

Army management control process. This regulation contains management control provisions according to AR 11–2 and contains a checklist for conducting management control reviews (see appendix F).

Supplementation. Supplementation of this regulation and establishment of command and local forms are prohibited without prior approval from the Deputy Chief of Staff, G–1, ATTN: (HQDA–MPA), 300 Army Pentagon, Washington, DC 20310–0300.

Suggested improvements. Users are invited to send comments and suggested improvements on DA Form 2028 (Recommended Changes to Publications and Blank Forms) directly to Deputy Chief of Staff, G–1 (DAPE–MPA), 300 Army Pentagon, Washington, DC 20310–0300. Naval personnel will provide their comments to Navy Recruiting Command, Operations Department (N35), Millington, TN 38054. Air Force personnel will send their comments to HQ, USAF/DPXET, 1040 Air Force Pentagon, Washington, DC 20330–1040. Marines will send their comments to Commandant Headquarters, U. S. Marine Corps, MCRC G-3 (Plans & Research), 3280 Russell Road, Quantico, VA 22134. Coast Guard will forward their comments to Commanding Officer, United States Coast Guard, 2300 Wilson Blvd., Suite 500, Arlington, VA 22201.

Committee Continuance Approval. The Department of the Army committee management official concurs in the establishment and/or continuance of the committee(s) outlined herein. AR 15-1 requires the proponent to justify establishing/continuing committee(s), coordinate draft publications, and coordinate changes in committee status with the U.S. Army Resources and Programs Agency, Department of the Army Committee Management Office (AARP-ZX), 105 Army Pentagon, Washington, DC 20310-0105.

---

*This regulaion supersedes AR 601-270/OPNAVINST 1100.4A/AFR 33-7/MCO P-1100.75A, dated 20 November 1999. This edition publishes a rapid action revision of AR 601-270/OPNAVINST 1100.4C/MCO 1100.75D/COMDTINST M 1100.2E.

Further, if it is determined that an established "group" identified within this regulation, later takes on the characteristics of a committee, as found in the AR 15-1, then the proponent will follow all AR 15-1 requirements for establishing and continuing the group as a committee.

Distribution. Distribution of this publication is available in electronic media only and is intended for command levels A, B, C, D and E for the active Army, the Army National Guard/Army National Guard of the United States, and the U.S. Army Reserve; Navy: Electronic media only; Air Force: F; USMC: PCN 10200590700; Coast Guard: Standard Distribution List No. 145; A: None; B: b(8); c(10); e(1); g(1); h(1); j(1); n(1); r(1); u(2); C: k(2); n(2); D: f(1); 1(1): E: None; F: None; G: None; H: None; Nonstandard

Distribution: C:t (Recruiting Offices). One to each office.

Contents (Listed by paragraph and page number)

Contents—Continued

Contents—Continued

Contents—Continued

Glossary

Chapter 1
Introduction

1–1. Purpose

a. Chapters 1 through 8 prescribe military entrance processing station (MEPS) operational policies and procedures applicable to recruiting activities of the military services and contain agency and command tasks for the operation and support of the MEPS.

b. Chapter 9 prescribes policies, procedures, and functions for the processing of Selective Service System (SSS) registrants. The primary mission of the MEPS is to—

(1) Provide aptitude testing and results, medically examine applicants in accordance with established physical standards prescribed in Department of Defense Instruction (DODI) 6130.4, and to perform background screening to ensure moral character provisions are met for enlistment in the military services according to the eligibility standards established by the services.

(2) Access into the military services those applicants accepted for enlistment or commissioning by the sponsoring military service.

1–2. References

Required and related publications and prescribed and referenced forms are listed in appendix A.

1–3. Explanation of abbreviations and terms

Abbreviations and special terms used in this regulation are explained in the glossary.

1–4. Responsibilities

a. In accordance with DODI 1304.8, the Department of Defense (DOD) Executive Agent for the Military Entrance and Processing Command (USMEPCOM) will be the Secretary of the Army (herein to as the Executive Agent).

b. The Under Secretary of Defense for Personnel and Readiness, (OUSD) (P&R) will have the operational, realignment and reorganization authority for USMEPCOM.

c. Secretaries of the Department of the Army, Air Force, and the Navy, (for the Navy and the Marine Corps) and the Secretary of the Department of Homeland Security, through the Commandant of the Coast Guard will—

(1) Provide military personnel to staff the MEPS during peacetime and mobilization. Also, finance related pay and allowance costs, including permanent change of station travel and temporary duty (TDY) travel for service-unique purposes.

(2) Finance of costs for transportation, meals, and lodging of applicants and enlistees.

(3) Furnish recruiting services examination and enlistment (Regular and Reserve Components, including the Delayed Entry Program (DEP) workload projections (fiscal year and quarterly) to the Deputy Assistant Secretary of Defense for Military Personnel Policy (DASD (MPP)/Accession Policy (AP)).

(4) Provide the DASD (MPP) (AP) with basic eligibility criteria for enlistment instructions used to prepare enlistment documents, assign enlistees, and distribute enlistment documents.

d. Army installation commanders are responsible for ensuring that Headquarters (HQ) USMEPCOM and subordinate units are provided the following:

(1) Personnel (Army and civilian only) and administrative services support (including legal and pay).

(2) Logistical support, except where interservice support is obtained from other military services, in accordance with DODI 4000.19.

e. Commanders of Army, Navy, Air Force, Marine Corps, Coast Guard, and Reserve Component recruiting activities will—

(1) Ensure that pertinent policies and procedures prescribed in this regulation are implemented uniformly.

(2) Provide quarterly recruiting objectives of each subordinate command (that is, brigade/battalion for Army or other service equivalent) to USMEPCOM Headquarters. The USMEPCOM staff will analyze these objectives and provide to sectors and MEPS for operational planning.

(3) Establish and maintain respective service-unique computerized job reservation systems located at each MEPS.

(4) Ensure the conduct and behavior of applicants and enlistees while being processed, to include behavior at meals and lodging facilities.

f. The Commander, USMEPCOM will command and control the sector headquarters and MEPSs. USMEPCOM is a jointly staffed DOD field operating activity under the Under Secretary of Defense for Personnel and Readiness (OUSD) (P&R). The Commander, USMEPCOM will—

(1) Establish and maintain the Command's Reporting System for reporting peacetime and mobilization induction and accession data, and related information in accordance with the DOD accession policy.

(2) Ensure professional and technical guidance is provided to MEPS chief medical officers (CMOs).

(3) Perform review and analysis, develop necessary plans and programs, and submit Defense Health Program (DHP) budget requirements to the U.S. Army Medical Command (MEDCOM).

(4) Perform review and analysis, develop necessary plans and programs, and submit budget requirements, other than DHP, to the Executive Agent.

(5) Establish and maintain MEPS facilities at locations prescribed by DASD MPP and develop facility layouts, space, and equipment requirements.

(6) Inspect all MEPS according to USMEPCOM Regulation 20–1.

(7) Develop MEPS workload capabilities (testing, medical examination, and processing), staffing patterns, and personnel requirements. Publish and distribute joint tables of distribution and allowance, or changes thereto, to appropriate agencies and activities.

(8) Maintain geographic boundaries for the MEPS military entrance test (MET) site and high school testing.

(9) Design, implement, sustain and operate the necessary automated enterprise data processing system to support DOD accession policy.

(10) Initiate requests, as necessary, to include inter-service support agreements (ISAs), where appropriate, to obtain services (to include legal services) and logistical support for MEPS activities.

(11) Maintain liaison with commanders of the recruiting services and training commands of the military Services, Surface Deployment and Distribution Command (SDDC), Office of the Chief of Engineers, the Department of Army Assistant Chief of Staff for Installation Management (ACSIM), U.S. Army Medical Command (MEDCOM), U.S. Army Signal Command (USASC), and Information Integration and Analysis Center. Also, maintain liaison with the Chief, National Guard Bureau (NGB); Administrator, General Services Administration; Director, Office of Personnel Management (OPM), Defense Finance and Accounting Service (DFAS), Director, SSS, and Defense Manpower Data Center (DMDC).

(12) Establish policies, procedures, specifications, and standards for requesting negotiation of meals and lodging contracts according to USMEPCOM Regulation 715–4. Provisions for meals and lodging of applicants and enlistees while at the MEPS and undergoing processing or waiting shipment after enlistment will be made on a contract basis, except to the extent that in-house lodging and dining facilities are available that do not require the services or products of a commercial firm.

(13) Establish policies, procedures, specifications and standards for transporting MEPS enlisted applicants to the services designated duty station.

(14) Establish and maintain procedures as a trusted agent to authenticate applicants' identity prior to enlistment.

g. Commanders of USMEPCOM sectors will—

(1) Exercise direct command authority, consistent with Headquarters' policy, over the operation of MEPS within their respective geographical areas of responsibility.

(2) Supervise the operation of MEPS to ensure established policies and procedures are accomplished effectively and efficiently.

(3) Monitor MEPS personnel facilities, equipment supplies, administrative services, and logistical support requirements.

(4) Furnish monthly workload projections to the MEPS and monitor the flow of applicants into the MEPS for examination and enlistment.

(5) Maintain liaison with appropriate counterpart service recruiting commanders/directors, SSS Headquarters Liaison, and directors of local OPM regions to ensure maximum cooperation in connection with MEPS matters of mutual concern.

Chapter 2
Functions of Military Entrance Processing Station and Recruiting Activities

2–1. Military entrance processing station functions
The functions of the MEPS are to—

a. Provide aptitude testing and medical examinations to applicants for accession into the active and Reserve components of the military service, including the United States Coast Guard; and provide the testing and examination results to the sponsoring service to identify applicants who meet the service, DOD mandated enlistment eligibility standards.

b. Enlist applicants accepted by the sponsoring military service.

c. Conduct quality review of enlistment documents prepared by MEPS and interview applicants for the purpose of assisting recruiting services in the prevention of fraudulent entry into the military services.

d. Prepare DD Form 4 series, (Enlistment/Reenlistment Document Armed Forces of the United States) in accordance with instructions from the Commander, USMEPCOM. Complete items 3 through 10 and 12 of DD Form 1966 series

(Record of Military Processing-Armed Forces of the United States) regarding acknowledgment of service obligation according to the instructions from the Commander, USMEPCOM.

e. Capture and forward fingerprints to designated agencies to initiate the entrance national agency check (ENTNAC)/national agency check (NAC)/national agency check with Local Agency and Credit Check (NACLC).

f. Submit all social security numbers (SSNs) to the Social Security Administration (SSA) and Alien Registration Numbers to the United States Citizenship and Immigration Services (USCIS) for verification (USMEPCOM requirement).

g. Prepare DD Form 93 (Record of Emergency Data), except for Coast Guard. For the Coast Guard use CG Form 4113 (Record of Emergency Data).

h. Prepare orders and amendments for travel of enlistees to initial training reception activities or other duty stations designated by the sponsoring service.

i. Publish initial active duty for training (IADT) or active duty for training (ADT) orders for RC personnel when requested by the respective service.

j. Assemble and distribute enlistment documents according to instructions contained in personnel procurement directives issued by the sponsoring service. Assembly and sequence of documents will be in accordance with USMEPCOM Regulation 601–23.

k. Arrange transportation for enlistees to local transportation terminals and onward movement to stations designated by the sponsoring service.

l. Conduct enlistment qualification testing at sites outside the MEPS according to policies and procedures prescribed in this publication, in AR 601–222, and by the Commander, USMEPCOM.

m. Provide arrangements for lodging, meals, and local transportation if applicable, for applicants and enlistees while they are undergoing processing at the MEPS. If it is necessary to procure these services from commercial facilities, such procurement will be accomplished only through the supporting contracting offices. Contracting officers will accomplish the procurement according to the appropriate Defense acquisition regulation.

n. Maintain accountability of services rendered by contractors and vendors, and submit payment according to procedures established by the Commander, USMEPCOM.

o. Conduct medical examinations of individuals who are non-enlistment applicants, upon request from a military service or other Federal activity. These examinations will not adversely affect the accomplishment of the primary mission. The sponsoring activity will obtain parental or legal guardian consent to the medical examination if required (see para 3–11). The examinations will be scheduled in advance through coordination with the MEPS. Costs incident to the medical examination, including specialty consultations and laboratory evaluations ordered by the MEPS physician, will be paid from USMEPCOM operating funds on a non-reimbursable basis, unless reimbursement provisions are specified.

p. Ensure complete, timely, and accurate preparation, collection, and transmission of the individual's examination and enlistment records and related data according to the procedures established by the Commander, USMEPCOM.

q. Ensure reservists and prior-service applicants provide appropriate release or separation documentation to properly process onto active duty (AD).

r. Conduct orientation briefings concerning the operation of MEPS for recruiting personnel as appropriate.

s. Conduct testing with the Armed Services Vocational Aptitude Battery (ASVAB) according to AR 601–222/Chief Naval Operations Instruction (OPNAVINST) 1100.5/AFJI 36–2016/Marine Corps order (MCO) 1130.52F/CG COMDTINST 1130.24A.

t. Perform accounting for appropriated funds, develop financial plans and programs, conduct financial review and analysis, and conduct management analysis to maximize operational efficiency in terms of funding resources.

u. Collect specimens and ship to DOD certified laboratories (selected and contracted by DOD) for Human Immunodeficiency Virus (HIV) Antibody initial screening and confirmation testing, as necessary.

v. Conduct alcohol testing by breathalyzer during pre-accession medical examinations at MEPS and confirm all positive readings. Collect urine specimens and ship to DOD certified laboratories (selected and contracted or ordered by DOD) for initial drug screening and confirmation testing, as necessary.

w. Ensure that applicants, registrants and enlistees receive, when necessary, medical attention for medical emergencies or injuries occurring at the MEPS according to USMEPCOM regulations.

x. Provide the Education Services Specialist to chair the Education Subcommittee of the Interservice Recruitment Committee.

2–2. Recruiting activity functions
The functions of local area recruiting activities are to—

a. Schedule applicants on a daily basis for medical examination, ASVAB testing, enlistment, meals, and lodging. Ensure the projected schedules support MEPS requirements for evenly distributed workload demands. Project enlistees to ship by the 15th of the month prior to the actual ship month; confirm shipper projections by name one working day prior to shipping.

b. Conduct preliminary screening of applicants to ensure those who are obviously physically unfit for military service (such as current history of epilepsy or diabetes), ineligible for ASVAB testing or retesting, or are non-English speaking, or not scheduled for an examination. The DD Form 2807–2 (Medical Prescreen of Medical History Report) will be completed by each individual who requires medical processing at the MEPS. The DD Form 2807–2 should be completed by the applicant with the assistance of the recruiter, parent(s), or guardian, as needed. Use of this form will also facilitate efficient, timely, and accurate medical processing of individuals applying for military service. The form is designed to assist recruiters in the medical prescreening of applicants. At a minimum, the DD Form 2807–2, once completed by the individual, will be submitted one processing day in advance, to the MEPS that is projected to process the individual. If support documentation (for example, private physician's paperwork, treatment records, consultations, and so forth) is required to augment the MEPS Chief Medical Officer review, a minimum of 2 processing days in advance is required, depending on the documentation; MEPS will inform service liaison of examinees' processing status following the completion of DD Form 2807–2. Applicants with prior service will submit all pertinent separation documents along with the DD Form 2807–2.

c. Ensure individuals with prior service submit a DD Form 214 (Certificate of Release or Discharge from Active Duty) member copy 4 (must indicate RE-codes), DD Form 215 (correction to DD Form 214) or NGB Form 22. If a Reenlistment Eligibility Data Display (REDD) Level 2 printout is used, then it must be submitted in accordance with USMEPCOM policy. In rare instances when the above documents have not been issued or the documents do not capture the most recent term of service; MEPS may accept a Discharge Order for processing prior service applicants. For those applicants who are currently serving in one of the services (Active or Ready Reserve) a DD Form 368 (Conditional Release) and supporting medical documents are required in lieu of the DD Form 214. These documents will be presented to the MEPS medical section for review with the DD Form 2807–2 in advance of the physical examination. The MEPS practitioner will determine if additional separation records are needed to afford or complete MEPS medical processing, as appropriate. The appropriate service medical waiver review authority may also request additional records.

d. Ensure all non-US citizens have a permanent resident card with a valid alien registration number.

e. Ensure noncitizen applications have a Lawful Permanent Resident card with a valid alien number for authentication.

f. Obtain parental or legal guardian consent for the medical examination(s) and review of medical record information of minors (para 3–11). Obtain parental or legal guardian signature certification on medical prescreening forms of minors (item 8 on DD Form 2807–2).

g. Arrange necessary transportation for applicants to the MEPS (or place of lodging when appropriate) or remote MET site and for return to their residence when applicable. During mobilization, the procedures outlined in chapter 9 apply.

h. Explain procedures that must be followed to receive meals and lodging at the contract facility. Explain that processing can be denied for applicants who violate the rules of conduct. Explain rules of conduct expected of applicants during their stay at contract lodging facilities, and provide each applicant with lodging information. The recruiting service will advise applicants of the services available at the lodging facility, including those for which a fee is chargeable to them. In the event that an applicant is identified as a suspect in a criminal offense occurring while processing or in the contract lodging facility, enlistment processing will be suspended pending completion of an investigation conducted by the local police. If the local police choose not to initiate an investigation, an inquiry by the recruiting service will be conducted. A copy of the findings will be provided to the MEPS Commander for review and consideration.

i. Assume responsibility for applicants/enlistees who, as a result of misconduct, medical emergency, family problem/emergency, legal problem, or any other problems not a direct result of MEPS processing, cannot continue processing or are delayed from shipping to their AD station.

j. Explain the processing procedures and ensure that applicants are properly prepared for the medical evaluation. This includes any information or pamphlet developed by USMEPCOM for distribution to the examinees. Ensure the applicant provides any medical records or documents regarding illness, hospitalization, injuries, treatment, or surgery, and so forth, that may be required or requested by the MEPS examining practitioner. Stress to applicants the importance of reporting for examination on schedule in a rested condition and in appropriate dress (para 3–6). Inform the examinees that the exam may take more than one day.

k. Identify applicants who require special examinations or testing necessary to determine qualification for specific enlistment programs. Furnish the name of the test site location and the date testing occurred when applicants have been previously tested on the student or enlistment ASVAB. Identify prior-service applicants and specify medical fitness standards to be applied. If no MEPS medical processing is required, obtain appropriate service waiver of MEPS medical processing and inform the MEPS.

l. Determine the eligibility of applicants for particular service programs, including enlistment grade or rank, according to the service personnel procurement directives.

m. Ensure applicants and enlistees with military training or school start date commitments are sent to the MEPS for shipment in a timely manner. Inform the MEPS Medical Section of any new medical information that was not previously disclosed and/or any interval medical history change since the time of the last MEPS medical evaluation and provide additional medical documentation to the MEPS as requested.

n. Furnish all applicable data necessary for preparation of assignment, travel, and AD orders for applicants scheduled to enlist.

o. Maintain enlistment documents pertaining to members of the U.S. Army Reserve Alternate Training Program (U.S. Army Recruiting Command only).

p. Forward necessary enlistment documents in sufficient quantities and sequence to the MEPS for distribution. Document assembly and sequence are identified in USMEPCOM Regulation 601–23.

q. Support the Student Testing Program prescribed in AR 601–222/OPNAVINST 1100.5/AFJI 36–2016/MCO 1130. 52F/CG COMDTINST 1130.24A.

r. Conduct officer direct commissioning program.

s. Attend the Recruiter Orientation conducted at the MEPS within 90-days of arrival, if assigned as a new recruiter.

t. Furnish all applicable enlistment waiver codes in items 17 and 18 of DD Form 1966 Series (Record of Military Processing–Armed Forces of the United States).

Chapter 3
Operational Guidance

3–1. Military Entrance Processing Station operations
MEPS will operate on a 5-day workweek, excluding Federal Holidays. Upon request of one or more of the recruiting services through the Inter-Service Recruitment Committee (IRC), Commander USMEPCOM may authorize the operation of MEPS on Saturdays. This will be dependent on mission requirements and funds available in coordination with the stakeholders. MEPS will not open during 3-day Federal holiday weekends.

3–2. Interservice Recruitment Committee
The IRC serves as the coordinating body through which harmonious relationships between local recruiting organizations and MEPS are maintained. The IRC will serve as a forum for the coordination discussion, and resolution of areas of mutual concern; however, it does not have the authority to make operational decisions for the MEPS.

a. Committee functions. The IRC considers all matters of mutual interest affecting the accomplishment of the recruiting and MEPS missions, to include—

(1) Coordination of all aspects of the Armed Services Student Testing Program, according to AR 601–222/ OPNAVINST 1230.lB/AFJI 36–2016/MCO 1130.52F.

(2) Dissemination of MEPS policies and procedures concerning enlistment qualification testing and the medical and administrative processing of applicants.

(3) Establishment of processing quotas, when required, and applicant projection requirements for the MEPS and MET sites. Reserve Components, to include the Army National Guard, whose recruiting service is separate from their Active Component will be entitled to a percentage of MEPS processing seats consistent with their percentage of total projected accessions for their respective service. Available processing seats not reserved may be used by either an Active or a Reserve Component on an as-needed basis.

(4) Exploration of procedures for more efficient processing of applicants.

(5) Exchange of data on projections, no-shows, walk-ins, medical pre-screening performance rates, pre-enlistment interview disclosures, recruiting production status and retest request, for the purpose of improving applicant processing procedures.

(6) Establishment of working level and ad hoc subcommittees, as required. Each IRC shall establish an education subcommittee composed of the MEPS Education Services Specialists (ESS) and Service Education Services Specialists or operations officers. This subcommittee will meet with the same frequency as the full IRC to discuss issues involving the Student Testing Program.

(7) Coordination of liaison activities with local and State educational officials, as required.

b. Committee's composition. There is an IRC at each MEPS. The IRC is composed of the commanders of the Army Recruiting Battalion, Army National Guard State(s) Recruiting and Retention Manager, Navy Recruiting District, Marine Corps Recruiting Station, Air Force Recruiting Squadron, MEPS and Recruiter-In-Charge of the Coast Guard Recruiting Office or Recruiting Detachment and MEPS. Reserve Components will be invited to IRC meetings as nonvoting members. The chair should be rotated on an annual basis among the voting members of the IRC. There is also an Education Subcommittee, chaired by the MEPS Education Service Specialist (ESS), to discuss and resolve Student Testing Program (STP) issues and brief the IRC at every meeting on those issues as well as the status of the STP.

c. Convening frequency. The IRC will formally convene not less than quarterly with more frequent meetings encouraged as necessary. Committee representatives of any military service can call a meeting of the committee at any time, consistent with prudent judgment and the availability of service representatives. The minutes of each IRC meeting will be recorded and distributed within 10 working days to each voting and nonvoting IRC member and each member of the appropriate Recruiting Commander/Operations Conference (RC/OC).

d. Duties of the IRC chairperson. The chairperson's duties include—

(1) Coordination of dates and locations for meetings as agreed upon by members.

(2) Establishment of the meeting agenda and schedule from input provided by members and representatives.

(3) Initiation of invitations, to appropriate organizations and individuals involved in any aspect of recruiting or MEPS matters, to attend meetings.

(4) Preparation and distribution of IRC minutes.

e. Voting. The IRC is ruled by majority vote. When practical, the Commander from each recruiting service and MEPS will attend IRC meetings. Each recruiting service member and each MEPS have one vote on matters before the committee. The MEPS commander is a voting member. Reserve Components are non-voting members and are represented during voting by their active service counterparts. Approval of the MEPS commander must be obtained on those matters concerning MEPS resources, capabilities, or mission. A dissenting service may forward the issue to the RC/OC.

f. Resolution of disagreements in the IRC. The IRC provides commanders of recruiting and processing activities a forum to raise and resolve issues affecting accomplishment of the recruiting mission and MEPS processing mission. It is expected that such issues will be resolved locally by direct coordination. When satisfactory resolution is not possible, referral to the RC/OC is appropriate. However, the IRC concept is not intended to abridge any commander's function and authority to accomplish assigned missions. If agreement cannot be reached by the IRC the military service that introduced the issue will document the committee action and forward the issue to the RC/OC for resolution. Issues which cannot be resolved by the RC/OC will be referred through HQ, USMEPCOM, ATTN: J–3/MOP to the stakeholders' meeting for resolution.

3–3. Recruiting Commanders/Operations Conference

The Recruiting Commanders/Operations Conference (RC/OC) provides interface between the functions of recruiting and processing above that of the local operational level. The objective of the RC/OC is to improve the working relationships among members and to enhance the mission accomplishment of the recruiting mission and MEPS processing missions. The RC/OC provides a continuing means of resolving those problems of policy implementation, coordination and standardization within the assigned geographic boundaries of RC/OC members.

a. Committee functions. The RC/OC will consider all matters of mutual interest affecting the accomplishment of the recruiting and MEPS missions, to include—

(1) Coordination of MEPS support requirement for the recruiting services located within the geographical boundary of each USMEPCOM sector.

(2) Exchange of recruiting and MEPS-related information of mutual interest.

(3) Resolving issues that could not be satisfactorily resolved at the local IRC operational level.

b. Committee's composition. There is a RC/OC for each sector. The RC/OC is composed of commanders of USMEPCOM sectors, Army recruiting brigades, Army National Guard national area recruiting managers, Navy regions, Air Force groups, Marine Corps districts, and Coast Guard regions. In addition, the following will be invited to attend and participate: equivalent level commanders of the Reserve Components; recruiting and retention advisory committee members; Chief, Air National Guard recruiting and retention branch (Air National Guard Readiness Center); and Coast Guard recruiting service personnel. The respective sector commander will be the chair. The RC/OC is normally organized along the geographical boundaries of the USMEPCOM sectors and will be identified by the sector designation, for example, Eastern Sector. Because of disparate boundaries, membership in more than one committee on the part of recruiting commanders may be required, and further subdivision is authorized to accommodate peculiar situations.

c. Convening frequency. The RC/OC will formally convene at least twice annually with more frequent meetings encouraged. Committee representatives of any military service can call a meeting of the committee at any time consistent with prudent judgment and the availability of the service representatives. Committees are encouraged to rotate locations of meetings with the services acting as hosts in their respective areas or in third-party locations such as training centers. The service that hosts the RC/OC meeting must provide clerical assistance for recording minutes of the meeting.

d. Duties of the RC/OC chairperson. The chairperson's duties include—

(1) Coordination of dates and locations of meetings as agreed upon by members.

(2) Establishment of the meeting agenda and schedule from input provided by members and representatives.

(3) Initiation of invitations to appropriate organization and individuals (involved in any aspect of recruiting or processing matters) to attend meetings.

(4) Preparation and distribution of RC/OC minutes to committee members and HQ USMEPCOM, ATTN: MOP.

e. Voting. The RC/OC is ruled by majority vote. When practical, the commander from each recruiting service, to include the National Guard, and USMEPCOM sector will attend the meetings. Each will have one vote on matters before the committee. When more than one recruiting service representative is a member, the senior officer present from that service will provide the vote for that service. Reserve Component representatives will be nonvoting members and represented during voting by their active service counterparts. Approval of the sector commander must be obtained in those matters concerning MEPS resources, capabilities, or mission.

f. Resolution of disagreements. In cases where agreement cannot be reached by the RC/OC, service dissents may be forwarded through HQ USMEPCOM, ATTN: J–3/MOP to the Stakeholders' meeting for resolution according to paragraph 3–4.

g. Information products. Sector commanders will keep voting and nonvoting RC/OC members abreast of MEPS matters through the transmittal of management data and operational policies, as required.

3–4. Stakeholders' meeting
The Stakeholders provide interface between the functions of recruiting and processing at the command level.

a. Committee functions. The Stakeholders will consider all matters of mutual interest affecting the accomplishment of the recruiting and USMEPCOM missions. Issues which cannot be satisfactorily resolved at the RC/OC level will be acted upon by the Stakeholders.

b. Committee composition. The committee will consist of the commanders of the recruiting services, Training Commands and the Commander, USMEPCOM.

c. Convening frequency. The Stakeholders meeting will formally convene at least once annually.

3–5. Training Commander/Operations Conference
The Training Commander/Operations Conference (TC/OC) provides interface between the functions of recruiting, reception/training and processing at the Operations Officer level.

a. Committee functions. The TC/OC will consider all matters of mutual interest affecting the accomplishment of the recruiting services, reception training centers and USMEPCOM missions. Issues identified at the RC/OC may be addressed at the TC/OC as well.

b. Committee composition.. The committee will consist of Operations Officers or their representatives from the Service Reception Training centers along with medical representatives, recruiting services HQ Operations Officers, MEPCOM sector representatives, HQs USMEPCOM MOP and MMD representatives.

c. Convening frequency. The TC/OC will formally convene at least once annually.

3–6. Scheduling of applicants
Applicants will be scheduled for processing, including ASVAB testing, on a by name and social security number (SSN) basis according to procedures established by HQ, USMEPCOM and in coordination with the IRC and local MEPS procedures. Examining and/or enlistment requirements and time of arrival will be furnished for each applicant by the appropriate recruiting service.

3–7. Applicant clothing standards
Applicants being processed at the MEPS will be dressed in a manner decided by the IRC. Applicants undergoing a medical examination or medical inspection will be required to wear underclothing (shorts for males and brassieres and underpants for females). Applicants who do not meet clothing standards will be denied processing and returned to the recruiting service liaison.

3–8. Military Entrance Test site projections
Projections by name, SSN, or number may be required, dependent upon HQ USMEPCOM and local MEPS standing operating procedures (SOPs) in conjunction with the IRC. At the Military Entrance Test (MET) sites not requiring projections, notification by the recruiting services to the MEPS will be made only when there will be no applicants for a specific session, or when the site capacity of 25:1 examiner/proctor ratio will be exceeded. Notification will be made to the MEPS no later than 1200 on the day prior to the session in question. For OPM-administered MET sites, the MEPS will notify OPM at a time determined by mutual agreement, on the day prior to canceled sessions.

3–9. Conduct of recruiting activities within the MEPS
Engagement in recruiting interviews with applicants is not authorized within the MEPS, meal and lodging facilities, MET sites, or during school testing. Recruiting activity may be conducted only in respective service guidance counselor or liaison offices.

3–10. Examination of applicants
Policies, functions, and procedures for the enlistment qualification testing and medical examination of applicants for enlistment, and related matters, are in chapters 7 and 8. Enlistment qualification testing or medical examination of an applicant without an SSN is not authorized. Testing or processing applicants for enlistment when they are in an

intoxicated condition (alcohol or drugs) is not authorized. MEPS will stop processing applicants that are belligerent or disrespectful to MEPS staff or other applicants during processing.

3–11. Processing of minors
The following guidance is provided to the MEPS when reviewing the DD Form 1966/5 (Section VI–Parental/Guardian Consent For Enlistment):

a. Parents or guardian(s) signature(s) are required to process a minor applicant for enlistment (for example, medical examination, enlistment). If only one parental signature can be reasonably obtained, it must be stated in accordance with service standards on DD Form 1966/5 (Section VI) why only one parent has signed the consent of minor enlistment. Medical examination is not authorized if either parent objects or if a legal guardian objects; the recruiting services will not project a minor applicant to process at the MEPS if a parent or guardian objects.

b. Minors with divorced parents require the signature of the parent assigned sole custody or, if joint custody was awarded, the signature of either parent.

c. It is the service's responsibility to complete item 40, "Verification of Single Signature Consent" statement on the DD Form 1966/5, which is necessary to explain why only one parent has signed the consent form. The medical examination is not authorized if this section is not completed, when required.

d. The applicant can file a petition in state court to be declared emancipated, which means the applicant legally becomes an adult at age 17. Attach any court document(s) regarding the emancipation to DD Form 1966/5 and process the applicant if otherwise eligible.

e. Marriage will automatically emancipate a minor applicant in most states. The recruiting service will only project such minors who are emancipated by marriage.

3–12. Public affairs
a. General. Examination and processing records accomplished or prepared at MEPS contain personal information and, therefore, will only be released to authorized personnel according to the Privacy Act of 1974 (section 522a, Title 5, United States Code (USC) and the Health Insurance Portability and Accountability Act of 1996 (Public Law 104–191)). The use of Government facilities and personnel for the purpose of compiling materials for use by commercial enterprises is prohibited.

b. News media interviews and/or photographs. Interviews with or photography of applicants and enlistees by news communications media are encouraged, provided—

(1) All media visits are coordinated with and approved by the USMEPCOM Public Affairs Officer and the MEPS commander.

(2) Applicants and enlistees fully understand they are not obligated to talk with media representatives but may volunteer to do so. All applicants and enlistees interviewed or prominently visually featured must have completed a release consent form, USMEPCOM Form 360–1–2–R–E, 1 Feb 1999, prior to the activity. The consent form will be maintained in the MEPS media file. Minors must have parent's or legal guardian's consent prior to participating.

(3) News media be instructed that the views expressed by the applicants or enlistees are their personal views and opinions and are not endorsed by any military service, USMEPCOM, or DOD.

(4) Requests for media visits or interviews with recruiting service personnel and/or applicants be coordinated in advance by the service chain of command with the HQ USMEPCOM Public Affairs Office. Interviews with recruiting service personnel and that service's applicants will take place in the service liaison area to avoid disruption of MEPS workflow. Requests for background film or video footage (B-roll) in MEPS common areas must be approved in advance.

(5) Interviews and photographs not be conducted while applicants (or enlistees) are actually engaged in medical examination and enlistment qualification testing. Simulation of medical examination and enlistment qualification testing may be made, with HQ, USMEPCOM Public Affairs Officer's prior approval. For example, a blood draw simulation should not show the applicant's face or other distinguishing characteristics.

(6) Photographs of applicants reflect personal dignity and decorum. News media representatives will not normally be permitted to photograph, film, or videotape an actual enlistment ceremony. However, the USMEPCOM Public Affairs Officer may approve exceptions, provided the photography does not disturb the conduct of the ceremony or reduce its dignity.

c. Visitors to MEPS. The general public, especially relatives and friends to applicants for enlistment, are encouraged to visit MEPS. They will not be permitted to visit processing and examining sections while in active operation. The enlistment ceremony is a meaningful event, both for the enlistee and their guests. Capturing the event through video or still photography is authorized to the extent practical. Oath of Enlistment officers will use discretion to ensure that photography is done so as not to interfere with the solemnity of the ceremony.

3–13. Requisition of Forms
Army, Air Force, Navy and Marines. Requisition and distribution of blank DOD, Department of the Army (DA), and standard form (SF) will be made according to AR 25–30 and DA Pamphlet 25–30, section I. Requisitions for necessary

forms issued by the Department of the Air Force, Department of the Navy, and Headquarters Marine Corps will be submitted according to AR 25–30.

3–14. Maintenance and disposition of files

MEPS files will be maintained and disposed according to AR 25–400–2. Documents relating to the examination of individuals will be maintained in the MEPS examination files located in a restricted access room. Access to the files room will be restricted to MEPS personnel on a "need-to-know" basis, as determined by the MEPS commander. These individuals will be designated, in writing, and this document must be posted at the files room entrance. The same applies for electronic files.

3–15. Release of information to Federal or State agencies

DOD and other federal agencies have reciprocal working relationships, whereby persons not qualified for military service may be referred to federal or state agencies for training, schooling, employment or rehabilitation opportunities. The MEPS will furnish medical results and enlistment qualification test scores when recruiting services request these scores for their referral purposes. The responsibility for obtaining consent from the applicant to release medical results and/or enlistment qualification scores rests with the sponsoring recruiting service.

3–16. Examination of non-English speaking applicants

Applicants for enlistment must comprehend English well enough to complete processing requirements. Applicants identified during ASVAB confirmation testing interviews, enlistment qualification testing, medical processing or MEPS pre-enlistment interviews as non-English speaking, will be referred to the section chief available (testing, medical, or operations officer) for evaluation. If indicated, a recommendation for the termination of processing will be submitted to the MEPS commander. If processing is terminated by the MEPS commander (or operation officer or test control officer), the notation "non-English speaking applicant Reevaluation Believed Justified (RBJ) after 90 days" will be recorded in the ASVAB score record, DD Form 2808 (Report of Medical Examination), DD Form 1966 Series, and USMEPCOM integrated resource system (USMIRS) as appropriate, and the applicant will be returned to the sponsoring service. Further enlistment processing will require a waiver of MEPS examination and/or interview requirements contained in this regulation. Waiver must be obtained through recruiting channels from the appropriate military department.

Chapter 4
Personnel

4–1. General

a. Administration of MEPS personnel will be governed by pertinent laws and regulations of the service in which they are members. Command control includes the authority and direction necessary for effective and efficient accomplishment of assigned functions.

b. Performance evaluation reports will be prepared according to directives issued by the respective services. Rating schemes will be published as directed by Commander, USMEPCOM.

c. Commander, USMEPCOM will administer military justice for military personnel assigned to USMEPCOM.

4–2. Staffing

MEPS will be staffed by military personnel of the military services and civilian employees provided by the Department of the Army, according to DOD Directive 1145.2.

4–3. Assignment qualifications

Assignment qualifications for officer and enlisted personnel are listed in appendix D.

4–4. Relief of unsatisfactory personnel

a. Military personnel assigned or attached to USMEPCOM whose personal conduct merits disciplinary action, or who are derelict in performance of duty, will be considered for expeditious relief or reassignment from USMEPCOM.

b. Procedures for relief of unsatisfactory personnel are listed below.

(1) MEPS commanders will—

(*a*) Initiate requests for relief according to service regulations and USMEPCOM policy.

(*b*) Inform the individual in writing of the contemplated relief action. If the relief is based upon a report of investigation or other written statements, furnish copies to the service member.

(*c*) Permit sufficient time, usually not more than 10 days, for the service member to rebut any comments or allegations. A negative reply will be required.

(d) Ensure Marine Corps and Navy personnel submit special fitness/evaluation reports according to service regulations.

(e) Prepare a letter to the sector headquarters with detailed statement of the circumstances leading to the request, including specific and typical instances of inadequate performances or a specific detailed description of a single significant event that precipitated the request. Also include a statement describing efforts taken to rehabilitate the individual. Provide a letter of notification to the individual as well as the individual's reply. Forward the request to the sector headquarters.

(2) Sector commanders will—

(a) Ascertain that the relief action is prepared according to this regulation and is administratively correct.

(b) Make a recommendation on the request pertaining to Navy and Marine Corps personnel, approve or disapprove the request on Army and Air Force Personnel.

(c) Forward the relief action request to HQ USMEPCOM, ATTN: J–1/MHR no later than 48 hours after receipt of the administrative review.

(3) The Commander, USMEPCOM will—

(a) Forward the request to the appropriate service.

(b) Request immediate reassignment of the relieved individual.

(c) Requisition a replacement when required.

(4) The service headquarters will assign a replacement expeditiously after notification of a relief action.

Chapter 5
Support Services

5–1. Activities

The Commander, USMEPCOM, will provide to both MEPS-assigned personnel and service liaison and guidance counselors assigned to each MEPS the following support services. The basis for determining the number of USMEPCOM-assigned personnel is the USMEPCOM Manning Authorization Document (UMAD). The basis for determining the number of service-specific counselor and liaison personnel is a service-specific manning document for each MEPS.

a. Office space, will be in conjunction with the Headquarters, Department of the Army (HQDA) (Assistant Chief of Staff for Installation Management (ACSIM)) or the General Services Administration. The square footage is determined by both the average applicant load at that MEPS and that MEPS' manning document. Each MEPS has an authorized square footage assigned to it by agreement with HQDA, ACSIM.

b. The Command's Reporting System network terminals and laser printers. Typically, each service's liaison office has one set of equipment provided to it within each MEPS. The integrated resource system (MIRS) is commonly known as an automated applicant processing system. No special or service-unique computer or network equipment will be provided by USMEPCOM.

c. Expendable supplies. Copier equipment will be procured by USMEPCOM for each MEPS for shared use by USMEPCOM-assigned and service liaison and counselor personnel physically located at each MEPS. Acquisition for copier equipment will be based on the combined copier volume generated by the MEPS and service liaisons and counselors. The copier size acquired will be based on actual workload and will be exclusively provided by and accounted for by HQ USMEPCOM using guidelines prescribed in AR 25–30. Copiers will be located throughout the MEPS for easy access by all users as determined by the MEPS commander.

d. Common furniture, other than that provided by USMEPCOM, is not authorized.

e. Telephone and limited data links.

5–2. Military Entrance Test site facilities

a. Facilities for the aptitude testing of applicants outside of the MEPS will be designated by the MEPS commander through coordination with voting and nonvoting members of the IRC, according to procedures prescribed by HQ USMEPCOM. The function for locating, identifying, and coordinating the use of facilities outside the MEPS will be shared by all members of the IRC. Procedures for the administration and protection of enlistment qualification tests are prescribed in USMEPCOM regulations and will be strictly followed. Provisions for travel of applicants while traveling to and from MET sites are the responsibility of the recruiting services. This responsibility includes providing meals.

b. The following standards will be used to provide adequate MET site facilities and equipment:

(1) Ensure suitable desks or tables and chairs for examinees. Writing surfaces will be flat and smooth. The space allotted to each individual must be wide enough to accommodate a test booklet and a separate answer sheet. Chairs with writing arms are not considered adequate for this purpose.

(2) Ensure freedom from distracting noises, properly illuminated, adequately ventilated, and maintained at a comfortable temperature.

(3) Ensure a secure storage area for electronic equipment and test materials.

Chapter 6
Operating Procedures

6–1. General
Plans for the efficient and orderly conduct of processing workloads, daily hire of fee-basis practitioners when needed, and meals, lodging, and transportation arrangements will be established based on the projections for examination and enlistment requirements furnished by the recruiting service. Consideration must be given to the overall workload requirements and arrival schedules. The recruiting services will make every effort to meet their projections. Processing of non-projected individuals will be at the discretion of MEPS Commander and in accordance with USMEPCOM policy.

6–2. Operating functions for MEPS commanders
MEPS Commanders will—

a. Supervise the total Command's Reporting System, to include the preparation and distribution of enlistment documents, forms, and military orders.

b. Establish procedures for the reception of applicants and ensure adherence to these procedures.

c. Establish and enforce procedures for safeguarding controlled testing materials, equipment and completed answer sheets.

d. Provide applicant examination results to sponsoring recruiting service.

e. Ensure a commissioned officer/warrant officer administers the Oath of Enlistment and signs the DD Form 4 series.

f. Ensure the enlisting officers delete enlistment data from the Command's reporting system for applicants that decline to take the Oath of Enlistment.

g. Ensure arrangements are made for the movement of enlistees from MEPS to reception or initial duty stations designated by the sponsoring recruiting service.

h. Monitor to ensure complete, timely, and accurate preparation and collection of applicant information is transmitted in accordance with DOD procedures on a daily basis to external agencies.

6–3. Applicant transportation
a. The sponsoring service functions include—

(1) Financing all costs incident to transportation and messing between the applicant's or enlistee's home and MEPS.

(2) Providing necessary transportation between the arrival terminal and lodging facility or the MEPS, unless provided by contract lodging facility.

(3) Providing round-trip transportation for those applicants sent to the MEPS for enlistment into the DEP or Reserve Components.

(4) Providing return transportation to the point of initial acceptance for applicants found disqualified for military service, those who are qualified but not enlisted, and those whose qualification status is yet to be determined.

(5) Providing transportation between the applicant's home and MEPS when the medical consultation is required but, cannot be performed on the same day as the medical examination and the applicant cannot be held over to receive the consultation the following day.

b. MEPS will furnish local transportation incident to the processing of applicants on a non-reimbursable basis between the MEPS and facility utilized for medical consultation. In accordance with USMEPCOM 715–4, Chapter 2–3a and b, transportation requirements between transportation terminals and the MEPS and to and from the lodging facility while undergoing processing at the MEPS will be included in the cost of lodging. No separate contract line item is required.

c. The sponsoring service will refer all eligible prior-service enlistees contemplating shipment of household goods, mobile homes, or privately owned automobiles to the transportation office of the supporting military installation or initial AD station.

d. If an enlistee absents himself or herself from the MEPS without authority prior to shipment or fails to appear for the departure of the enlistee's transportation, the MEPS will notify the recruiting service and the projected unit of assignment. Initiation of disciplinary, separation or apprehension action, if appropriate, is a function of the initial receiving activity or recruiting service; these actions are not responsibilities of MEPS.

e. The sponsoring service will take responsibility of accessed applicants that are delayed transportation at the request of the service.

6–4. National agency check with local check

a. Recruiting services are responsible for the preparation of the Standard Form 86 (Questionnaire for National Security Positions). Preparation can be manual or by using the DOD approved electronic version of the SF 86 (Electronic Personnel Security Questionnaire).

b. Recruiting services are responsible for receiving national agency check with local check (NACLC) security background investigation results from background investigation agency.

c. The MEPS is responsible for—

(1) Electronically transmitting fingerprints daily to the appropriate background investigation agency.

(2) Providing results of FBI fingerprint searches to the respective service as they become available.

6–5. MEPS pre-enlistment interview

MEPS will interview applicants (before the Oath of Enlistment is administered to DEP applicants and Reserve and National Guard accessions) for the purpose of assisting recruiting activities in preventing fraudulent entry into the military services. Any additional information obtained from applicants which may have a bearing on their qualifications for military service will be furnished to the appropriate MEPS officer and/or sponsoring recruiting service for resolution. Specific interview requirements and procedures will be established by the Commander, USMEPCOM, in coordination with recruiting service commanders.

6–6. MEPS pre-accession interview

MEPS will interview applicants in a manner similar to that of the pre-enlistment interview for a quality check before enlistment in an Active component from a DEP status. The pre-accession interview does not apply to Reserve and National Guard enlistees returning to MEPS for shipping. Additional interview requirements and procedures beyond those of the pre-enlistment interview will be established by the Commander, USMEPCOM, in coordination with recruiting service commanders.

6–7. Oath of Enlistment

a. The Oath of Enlistment will be administered in an auspicious, dignified ceremony, conducted only in the English language by the enlisting officer. Provisions for administrative discharge due to fraudulent entry and the general meaning of the Uniform Code of Military Justice (UCMJ) article 83 (Fraudulent Enlistment or Appointment) will be explained before the ceremony, along with DOD separation policy concerning restrictions on personal conduct in the military services. UCMJ article 85 (Desertion) and UCMJ article 86 (Absent without leave) will be explained before shipping. In accordance with section 502, Title 10, United States Code (10 USC 502), any commissioned officer of the armed forces may administer the Oath of Enlistment. No exceptions to this statutory requirement will be granted. Each person will be advised that he or she has the option to swear or affirm and that the words "so help me God" may be omitted.

b. Applicants will not be permitted to sign the DD Form 4/1, 4/2 and 4/3 (Enlistment Agreement) prior to the oral administration of the oath. The enlistment agreement is legally binding after the oath has been taken, notwithstanding the applicant's failure to sign. If the applicant refuses to sign the enlistment agreement after administration of the Oath of Enlistment, the enlisting officer will so note on the enlistment agreement and return the applicant to the sponsoring recruiting service where the matter will be resolved according to recruiting service policies.

6–8. Enlistment and travel orders

The recruiting services provide MEPS with the necessary information required for the preparation of enlistment, travel, and AD orders. For all non-prior service applicants, MEPS will use a standardized orders format prescribed by the Commander, USMEPCOM. Orders and amendments to orders for prior service enlistees will be prepared according to appropriate service directives.

6–9. Movement of enlistees

a. Policy and procedures for the movement of personnel are contained in the DTR 4500.9–R, Defense Travel Regulation. The recruiting services provide for the proper scheduling of individuals for MEPS enlistment and AD processing so the individuals' movement to training installations is accomplished in a timely manner. Consideration will be given to passenger standing route orders (PSRO), reception processing, and training and school start schedules.

b. PSROs issued by SDDC, in coordination with each MEPS, will govern the travel of enlistees to initial duty stations. The PSRO prescribes the mode of transportation, carrier, time, and route for repeated travel between two points. The following principles are applicable in establishing and executing a PSRO:

(1) Enlistee travel will not be scheduled between 2400 and 0600 hours. PSROs will be arranged for the enlistees so that any wait at a transportation terminal will not exceed 3 hours, wherever possible.

(2) The mode of transportation specified in the PSRO will be the most economical among the available routings and within the time constraints in (1) above. The cost of delay in commencing travel (including meals, lodging, lost

productive time, and necessary expenses en route) are factors to be added to the basic fare in comparing the economy of various modes.

(3) Although any overnight travel should be utilized only on rare occasions, enlistees traveling overnight by rail will be provided sleeping accommodations. Overnight travel by air or bus will not be used without authorization from HQ USMEPCOM. However, local problems which arise during processing remain the prerogative of the MEPS Commander to solve on an as needed basis.

6–10. Processing special category applicants

Special category applicants, as defined by USMEPCOM require special processing consideration.

a. The MEPS commander, in concert with the IRC membership, will establish policies to offer special category processing (by appointment) which is consistent with HQ USMEPCOM policy.

b. The sponsoring service will select the type of processing desired for its special category applicants. To receive special category processing, the service must coordinate with the MEPS medical section before projecting the applicant. The recruiting service will project the applicant as a special category processor on the USMEPCOM Form 727–E (Processing List) in accordance with local MEPS policies and will assign a service sponsor.

Chapter 7
Enlistment Qualification Testing

7–1. Authorization, control and administration of the Armed Forces Vocational Aptitude Battery

a. Policy is prescribed in AR 601–222 for the DOD enlistment, student and overseas testing programs.

b. HQ, USMEPCOM, as the DOD operating agency, has the function for publishing regulations or pamphlets prescribing operational procedures for the DOD enlistment, student and overseas testing programs.

c. The USMEPCOM published regulations will—

(1) Be applicable to all military recruiting services, MEPS, and users of MEPS facilities, including MET sites.

(2) Ensure quality control standards are met according to applicable directives.

(3) Be provided to all service accessions policy agencies and recruiting headquarters.

7–2. Exceptions to policy

Services requesting exceptions to policy will direct the request to their respective service representative on the Joint Service Manpower Accession Policy Working Group (MAPWG).

7–3. Requests for controlled test materials

a. Reproduction of controlled testing materials governed by this regulation is prohibited without the prior written approval of HQ, USMEPCOM (J–3/MOP TD).

b. At no time will controlled testing material, or information extracted there from, be released to any individual or agency not authorized access to such materials. Individual test scores will not be released to any non-MEPS individual or agency except as otherwise authorized.

c. Agencies requesting release of test materials or scores, as an exception to policy, will forward such requests in writing and through channels to HQ USMEPCOM, ATTN: J–3/MOP TD, who will forward as appropriate to Deputy Under Secretary of Defense (Military Personnel Policy) for review and approval/disapproval. The request will include—

(1) A statement of the reason for the "need to know."

(2) Anticipated use of test scores or testing material.

(3) The number and types of test scores or testing materials desired.

(4) Safeguard procedures to be used for controlling and protecting the test materials, test scores and names of examiners involved.

7–4. Unauthorized use of controlled test materials/data

a. Until an appropriate investigation is concluded, military, DOD civilians and contract test administrators will be suspended from testing duties whenever credible information or reports of an investigation reveal that they may have—

(1) Furnished controlled test material, test questions or answers to an unauthorized person.

(2) Been derelict in connection with protecting test materials.

(3) Been found with unauthorized possession of test materials.

b. If warranted, the individual will be referred to the commander or supervisor for consideration of appropriate disciplinary action under the UCMJ, DA or OPM regulations.

7–5. Overseas Enlistment Testing Program

a. The military services are responsible for operation of the Overseas Testing Program, in accordance with AR 601–222.

b. Commander, USMEPCOM will provide support to the overseas testing areas by designating specific MEPS to support testing outside of the Continental United States.

(1) The designated MEPS will—

(a) Enter applicant test data from the USMEPCOM Form 680–3A–E (Request for Examination) into the computerized records system.

(b) Determine if the Armed Forces Qualification Test (AFQT) scores indicate a need for confirmation testing.

(c) Determine if inappropriate retesting took place.

(2) HQ USMEPCOM will work issues regarding testing policy procedures and responsibilities with the Military Services Overseas Program Managers.

7–6. Special purpose testing

Special purpose tests are given at the request of the services to determine qualification of applicants for specific occupational specialties or special enlistment programs. MEPS are authorized to administer the tests listed in appendix C and additional tests approved by MAPWG. Special purpose tests may not be administered at MET sites.

7–7. Processing of applicants with nonqualifying scores

Applicants tested at MET sites who fail to obtain minimum requirements as established by the sponsoring service will not be sent to the MEPS for further processing. If circumstances prevail where an applicant is in medical processing and the test scores reveal that the applicant has not met service standards, the medical processing will continue.

Chapter 8
Medical Examinations

8–1. General

Medical examinations of applicants forwarded by the recruiting services and Selected service registrants will be accomplished under MEPS control. The quality of medical examinations will not be compromised for any reason. When required, MEPS medical personnel may request specialty consultations and other medical services; these consults and/or services will be obtained from other military, federal, or civilian medical facilities. However, the MEPS physician makes the final determinations of the applicant's and registrant's medical qualification for military service. Applicable charges for consultation services are payable from Defense Health Program (DHP) funds made available to USMEPCOM when said consults are obtained for the purposes of determining whether or not an applicant meets qualification standards or if requested by Service Medical Waiver Authority in order to make a waiver determination. Payment for services provided by Federal agencies will be made according to charge statements provided for this purpose.

8–2. Medical fitness standards

The medical standards for initial appointment, enlistment and induction are found in DODI 6130.4, less height, weight, and body fat standards which are administrative in nature, service-specific and are contained in applicable service publications and posted on the USMEPCOM Intranet. The standards for prior-service enlistees may be the initial entry standards or retention standards in accordance with applicable service guidelines.

a. Non-prior service males and females. Medical fitness standards for initial appointment, enlistment or induction in the military services are prescribed by DODI 6130.4. All services will develop service-specific guidance consistent with this DODI.

b. Prior service males and females. Medical fitness standards for prior-service personnel are prescribed in the publications listed for the following services:

(1) *Army.* AR 40–501, chapter 3, applies if reenlistment is accomplished within 6 months of discharge from active duty Army or if the individual is a current member of a USAR or ARNG unit (see AR 601–210, chap 3, table 3–1). Current drilling members of the USAR and ARNG may be processed and projected as "No Medical Required". These members must have a physical that is within 5 years of application for enlistment onto AD. All other applicants must meet the procurement standards of AR 40–501, chapter 2.

(2) *Navy and Marine Corps.* NAVMED P-117, Navy's Manual of the Medical Department (MANMED), chapter 15 as applicable.

(3) *Air Force.* AFI 48–123, attachment 2 applies to all individuals who have separated from AD with any of the regular Armed Services, but who are reenlisting in the regular Air Force or the Air Force Air Reserve Components (ARC) when no more than 6 months have elapsed between separation and reenlistment.

(4) *Coast Guard.* COMDTINST M1020.8F.

8–3. Medical examination of a minor
Requirements for obtaining parental or guardian consent to the medical examination of a minor are contained in paragraph 3–11. The recruiting services must ensure that the documentation for the processing of minors meets established service standards and is supplied to the MEPS before medical and/or enlistment processing begins.

8–4. Performing the medical examination
Medical examinations will consist of a medical history and clinical evaluation, laboratory findings, and other measurements and findings, as prescribed in DODI 6130.4 and USMEPCOM Regulation 40–1. Further evaluation may be required to ascertain whether an applicant meets special requisites for enlistment under certain programs. Prior-service applicants will be medically examined as required by the respective services. Item numbers specified in this section refer to item numbers on the DD Form 2808, unless otherwise noted.

8–5. Preparation for physical examinations
Since parts of the medical examination require the examinees to undress to undershorts for men and bra and underpants for females, all examinees must have these items when reporting for examination. When required to undress, provisions will be made for securing clothing. Personal items, such as watches and billfolds, will be retained by the applicant (on his or her person) or at the applicant's option, placed in a locker. Gowns will be provided for females. A MEPS female technician will always be present when female applicants are undergoing the physical examination and are undressed.

8–6. Examining practitioner evaluation
Clinical evaluations and diagnostic determinations are a responsibility of the examining practitioner under supervision of the Chief Medical Officer. These responsibilities will not be further delegated. The examining practitioner will carefully evaluate medical history information furnished by the applicant and provide a detailed summary in item 30, DD Form 2807–1. These responsibilities will not be further delegated. Orthopedic/neurological screening, designed to conduct en masse evaluation of an applicant's strength, mobility and coordination will not exceed six applicants per examining practitioner. A thorough examination which meets the same objectives of the orthopedic/neurological examination may be accomplished on an individual basis when feasible or practical. Applicants will be scheduled to allow sufficient time for thorough evaluation by the examining practitioner. Routine tests and measurements will be performed by enlisted or civilian medical technicians.

8–7. Clinical evaluation (general)
The clinical evaluation comprises items 17 through 72 of DD Form 2808. The examining practitioner will consider each step of the clinical evaluation individually and carefully and make proper judgment by using accepted medial principles and procedures in conducting the medical examination.

8–8. Orthopedic evaluation
This examination consists of specific movements, maneuvers and positions designed to detect abnormalities in posture and gait, limitations of joint motion, deformities, lack of muscle strength, impairment of coordination atrophy, absence of muscle or digits, skin abnormalities, scars and other abnormalities (see USMEPCOM 40–1). It will be conducted in a well-lit room so as to permit clear observation. Male applicants will remove all clothing except undershorts. Female applicants will remove all clothing except bra and underpants. If conducted en masse, the series of movements comprising the orthopedic/neurological examination may be demonstrated by an enlisted or civilian technician, but will be observed closely by a physician for abnormalities. The physician will properly evaluate and annotate all abnormalities.

8–9. Psychiatric evaluation
The mere possibility that a psychiatric condition will arise later in military service should not be sufficient reason, in itself, for disqualification; however, such a possibility should be considered in light of other findings (such as conviction of juvenile court or adjudication of serious offenses, drug abuse history, and other background information made available to the chief medical officer) and DOD and USMEPCOM policy and guidance.

8–10. Laboratory, measurements, and other findings
   a. Miscellaneous data fields. Unless specifically required, DD Form 2808 items 47, 48, 52a, 56, 59, 60, 62, 64, 65, 67, 68, 69, 70, and 72, will not be routinely completed by the MEPS, unless required by USMEPCOM 40–1. Only MEPS medical staffs are authorized to make entries on the DD Form 2807–1 and DD Form 2808. Prerecording of any findings on DD Form 2808, before factual results are known, is not authorized.
   b. Urinalysis. Urine reagent strips will be used to routinely determine the sugar and protein content of urine and annotated in items 45a and 45b.
   c. Height and weight. The individual's height will be measured barefoot and recorded in inches as prescribed by

service regulation. Weight will be measured in undershorts for men and bra and underpants for females and recorded as prescribed by service regulation. When required by the applicable service, body fat content will be determined and recorded in item 55 on the day of the initial physical exam.

d. Pulse and blood pressure. Pulse and blood pressure will be routinely accomplished in a sitting position, in accordance with USMEPCOM Reg 40–1 and recorded in items 57 and 58 of the DD Form 2808.

e. Vision. The Armed Forces Vision Test (AFVT) will be used for testing vision. Instructions for use of this instrument are contained in the instruction manual. If an applicant wears vision correction devices, their specific refraction will be determined by use of the auto refractor. The use of the lens-measuring instruments is no longer acceptable in accordance with USMEPCOM/MMD policy. Any further testing, to include manifest refractions, will be done in accordance with USMEPCOM Reg 40–1. Depth perceptions using the AFVT, will be conducted as required by USMEPCOM 40–1, but are not considered disqualifying for entry into the Armed Services.

f. Color vision. Although there is no current DODI standard for color vision, the Pseudoisochromatic Plates (P/P) color vision test will be administered to all examinees. Army applicants who fail the P/P test will be administered a red/green color vision test, either with the Farnsworth Lantern color perception test (FALANT) or by the Armed Forces Vision Tester or other means as prescribed by USMEPCOM 40–1. All Navy, Marine Corps and Coast Guard applicants will be further tested with the FALANT. No other tests besides the P/P test for color vision are authorized for Air Force applicants.

g. Hearing. Hearing tests will be accomplished by use of the automatic audiometers in sound-treated booths. Booths and audiometers must be calibrated according to current directives.

h. Pregnancy testing. Pregnancy testing will be performed on all female applicants during all physical examinations and all physical inspections incident to enlistment and reenlistment. Initial results will be recorded in block 46. Repeat tests will be recorded in block 73 or 80, along with the height, weight and body fat, if appropriate.

8–11. Summary of defects and diagnoses

Based on the clinical examination, significant medical defects, whether disqualifying or not, will be summarized in DD Form 2808, item 77, as prescribed by USMEPCOM 40–1. These diagnoses will be as specific and detailed as possible. Statements such as "disqualified for cardiovascular disease," "disqualified; psychiatric case," and so forth, are too general to be of value and should be avoided. The part or parts of the body affected will be specified whenever the diagnosis is not sufficient to localize the condition, as in cases of amputation, paralysis, aneurysm or ulcers. Manifestations or symptoms of a condition should not be used instead of a diagnosis, except in those cases where definite diagnosis is not possible or feasible without extensive or expansive consultation. When needed, extension of comments in this block should be continued in block 88.

8–12. Physical profile

Item 74b will be competed by the MEPS Chief Medical Officer or a supervised fee-basis physician who has privileges to profile. Utmost care will be taken to ensure accurate entries under the physical profile. The MEPS profile is an accession profile implying an applicant has met accession standards and is not necessarily equivalent to a fitness for duty profile used by the Army or Air Force for its members.

8–13. Qualification for military service

The applicant's qualifications for military service will be indicated in item 74a. All findings will be evaluated in terms of the standards prescribed in paragraph 8–2 of this regulation. If the applicant were found qualified, even though defects were stated in item 77, he or she will be informed of his or her medical fitness for military service. When applicable and in accordance with USMEPCOM policy, the DD Form 2808 will be reviewed to ensure that additional requirements of the policy sponsoring service, or requirements necessary to ascertain whether the applicant meets special requisites for specific enlistment programs have been accomplished. When an applicant is found to be medically unfit for military service, he or she will be informed by the examining physician concerning the disqualifying condition. If the condition is potentially progressive and requires further evaluation and/or treatment, the applicant will be advised to seek the services of a family physician or local health agency. The applicant will sign in item 75 reflecting the fact that the applicant has been informed of the condition requiring further evaluation. Additionally, the appropriate timeframe for follow-up will be circled. Applicants whose medical fitness cannot be immediately determined will be advised that they will be informed of their qualification for military service by the sponsoring recruiting service.

8–14. Signature

The practitioner who performed the medical history will sign item 82. The profiling physician will sign line 84. If a practitioner different from the profiling physician completed any other portion of the examination, he or she will sign in item 82. The Chief Medical Officer or other profiling physician will sign in item 84 after the applicant has been profiled and the examination completed. The typed, stamped or printed name of the physician will precede the signature.

8–15. Reproduction of DD Form 2808 and DD Form 2807–1

Completed and signed DD Form 2808 and DD Form 2807–1 will be reproduced in the required number of copies, using suitable reproduction equipment to provide legible, permanent copies. Any copies of the above forms, made prior to completion of the physical qualification process, will be clearly marked as working copies. These copies are not acceptable for inclusion into the applicant's final package which is sent to the recruit training centers.

8–16. Physical inspection

Applicants for enlistment and individuals processing through a MEPS under a commissioning program who have undergone a medical examination of the prescribed scope within 2 years and who have been found qualified, will undergo a physical inspection when processing for entry on AD or ADT in the military services, if more than 72 hours has elapsed from the initial examination or from a subsequent inspection. When processing for entry into the DEP or into the Reserve and National Guard (unless for ADT), if more than 30 days has elapsed from the initial examination or from a subsequent inspections, a physical inspection will be done. A physical inspection is not required for individuals entering on AD under a commissioning program and when authorized to proceed from school or their home directly to a duty station.

8–17. Medical reexamination

An applicant previously found qualified for military service will undergo a complete medical examination prior to enlistment, induction or appointment (commissioning) if more than 24 months have elapsed since the last complete examination was accomplished. The date of the last examination is the date shown in Item 1 of DD Form 2808. Applicants appearing for reexamination because of previous disqualification for a remedial or temporary medical condition will undergo a physical inspection if the previous examination was conducted within 2 years. The physical inspection will place emphasis on the previously disqualifying defect. The MEPS commander may, in consultation with the CMO, authorize medical reexamination when findings reflected on a previous DD Form 2808 and/or DD Form 2807–1 are inconsistent or in conflict with findings noted during the physical inspections. Portions of the examination may need to be repeated or re-evaluated as appropriate. If an individual who has already reported to initial entry training and was separated and returns to the MEPS within two years to again attempt access into a military service, the physical examination will be repeated with the former examination becoming an attachment to the reexamination. Separation documentation will be provided to the MEPS as requested and in accordance with HQ USMEPCOM policy.

8–18. Doubtful medical fitness cases

Final determination of an applicant's medical fitness for military service will normally be made by the MEPS CMO on the basis of the examination conducted at the MEPS. Whenever there is doubt as to whether or not an applicant meets the minimum medical requirements for military service, determination of acceptability can be made by the USMEPCOM Command Surgeon or other HQ USMEPCOM physician in accordance with USMEPCOM policy. The final determination will be recorded in Item 74a (and Item 74b and Item 76 as appropriate) of the DD Form 2808 with proper authentication.

8–19. Use of DA Form 1811

Applicants for enlistment in the U.S. Army who are reenlisting after a break in service that does not exceed 6 months may use DA Form-1811 (Physical Data and Aptitude Test Scores Upon Release from Active Duty) in lieu of a medical examination, provided there has been no change in the individual's physical condition since separation, no new diseases or injuries have been acquired, and the individual signs a statement to that effect. The applicant will prepare a DD Form 2808, enter in the Item 73 "Notes" section the following statement: "I have (have not) had any new diseases or injuries since my separation physical examination, and there has been no change in my medical condition" and sign the statement. A medical inspection will be accomplished and entries made in Item 77. If an exception is noted, a complete medical history and examination will be accomplished.

Chapter 9
Processing of Selective Service System Registrants

This chapter will be implemented upon direction of the Secretary of Defense.

Section I
General

9–1. Purpose of chapter

This chapter prescribes policies, procedures, and functions for processing Selective Service System (SSS) registrants for induction into the military services.

9–2. Functions

Agency and command functions for the operation and support of MEPS activities are prescribed in paragraph 1–4. Additional functions pertinent to induction processing are listed below.

a. The OUSD (P&R) will submit military induction requirements to the Director, SSS.

b. The Executive Agent will develop and promulgate—

(1) Induction plans, program requirements, policies, and procedures in coordination with DOD agencies; the Director, SSS; and other Federal activities, as appropriate.

(2) Programs, budgets and finances MEPS operating costs incident to the examination and induction of registrants. (The responsibility for costs incident to transportation meal, and lodging requirements for individuals in registrant status is prescribed in para 9–4.)

c. Mobilization personnel requirements. Services currently accepting personnel for induction will—

(1) Submit fiscal year and monthly induction estimates to OUSD (P&R).

(2) Submit, through Defense Manpower Data Center (DMDC) to the SSS, lists of personnel separated from the respective services prior to completion of their military obligation.

d. The Commander, USMEPCOM will—

(1) Maintain liaison with the National Headquarters, SSS and major training activities of the military services.

(2) Establish and maintain an automated induction system for reporting registrant examination results, inductee accession data, processing the SSS Delivery List and related information, as required.

(3) Furnish MEPS daily workload capacity and flow patterns, for registrant processing purposes, to the National Headquarters, SSS.

e. The MEPS commander will—

(1) Ensure examination of SSS registrants and determines their medical, aptitude, moral, and administrative qualifications for military service.

(2) Ensure induction of qualified registrants into military service as allocated by OSD.

(3) Arrange transportation for inductees to duty designated by the respective service.

(4) Submit registrant examination results and inductee accession information via the Command's Reporting System.

(5) Maintain liaison and coordinates activities with SSS MEPS Liaison Personnel (MLP).

f. SSS MEPS Liaison Personnel (MLP) will—

(1) Serve as the representative assigned by SSS to a designated MEPS.

(2) Serve as a liaison to the MEPS commander on all SSS related matters or problems that arise during the processing of SSS registrants, and perform the duties prescribed according to the latest USMEPCOM–SSS memorandum of understanding.

9–3. Concept of operations

The Selective Service System will operate in either of two methods. In the "One Step Mode", SSS will deliver a fixed number of registrants to each MEPS daily. The MEPS will process them by administering the ASVAB, conducting the physical examination and inducting them into their respective services. The MEPS will arrange transportation for inductees to their respective service training sites. Registrants who have filed claims for reclassification which are pending before a Selective Service Board or registrants not qualified due to medical, moral or other reasons will be returned home pending disposition of their case. In the "Two Step Mode", SSS will deliver a fixed number of registrants to each MEPS daily to have their aptitude, medical, moral, and administrative qualifications determined. The MEPS will process them as in the "One Step Method". All registrants will then return home. They will return to the MEPS for induction at a later date as determined by SSS and the respective services. During the interim, medical or moral problems will be adjudicated.

9–4. Transportation, meals, and lodging

Policies and procedures for the use of contract facilities and the control and accounting of services rendered by contract vendors are prescribed in paragraphs 1–4*f*(12). Policies and procedures contained in paragraph 6–9 concerning the movement of enlistees are also applicable to inductees. The responsibility for budgeting and financing transportation meals and lodging requirements for registrants and inductees is as follows:

a. Registrants. The SSS will provide registrants with travel warrants for transportation to the MEPS. MEPS personnel will assist registrants in completing SSS travel claim forms for reimbursement of unanticipated expenses and will mail them to the SSS for processing. Listed below are the categories of travel and the agencies accountable for providing travel assistance:

(1) From residence to MEPS–SSS.

(2) While at MEPS–USMEPCOM.

(3) Return to residence when found disqualified for service (including those found disqualified due to temporary or remedial conditions)–SSS. Registrants completing the examination under the two-step process will be provided a

charter bus run by SSS. Registrants who are returned to residence under the one-step process will be provided travel by the MEPS with reimbursement by SSS.

(4) Sent for examination only (from residence to MEPS and return to residence)–SSS.

(5) When qualifications for service are undetermined (this status will only be used for those registrants that remain under the physical control of the MEPS for three days or less)–USMEPCOM. If the registrant's qualification cannot be determined within three working days the registrant will be considered temporarily unacceptable for service and returned to residence–USMEPCOM with reimbursement by SSS.

b. Inductees. The responsibility for arranging the necessary transportation meals, and lodging for registrants, inductees, and enlistees is as follows:

(1) *Registrants.*

(a) From residence to MEPS–SSS.

(b) While at MEPS–MEPS, with reimbursement by SSS.

(c) From MEPS to residence–MEPS.

(2) *Inductees.* The MEPS.

(3) *Enlistees.* Service for which the individual is enlisting.

Section II
Administrative Processing Prior to Induction

9–5. SSS delivery list
The SSS delivery list is an alphabetical listing of registrants ordered to report for induction processing. It is prepared by the SSS and electronically transmitted to USMEPCOM as required. USMEPCOM in turn transmits the list to the MEPS 10 days prior the registrant's scheduled reporting date. The list contains the date the induction processing orders were issued and the date and time each registrant is scheduled to report for induction processing. It also contains each registrant's full name, and SSN, if available. Conscientious objectors are identified by codes as are registrants ordered for examination only or being rescheduled for processing.

9–6. Reception of registrants
Registrants reporting to MEPS are initially received by MEPS personnel. The tasks to be performed at the initial reception area include collecting orders to report for induction, posting the SSS delivery list, and determining if registrants have a problem requiring SSS MEPS Liaison Officer (MLO) involvement. Registrants will also be given an orientation briefing that will cover the processing steps, meals and lodging arrangements while at the MEPS, instructions for completing travel reimbursement requests where applicable, and conditions under which they will be released from the MEPS.

9–7. Volunteers for induction
Persons between the ages of 18 and 26 who have not completed their AD obligation under the Military Selective Service Act may volunteer with the SSS for induction. Persons between the ages of 17 and 18 may volunteer for induction with the consent of the parent or guardian. This is contained on the Application for Voluntary Induction, and will be considered as consent to medical examination.

9–8. Registrants with prior service
Registrants on the SSS delivery list who can verify prior-service when they report to the MEPS will be referred to the SSS MLP for clarification of their status. Reenlistment eligibility (RE) codes which are not disqualifying for induction are listed at table 9–1. The respective service will update this table accordingly. recruiting services need to validate these lists. RE codes not listed in table 9–1 are disqualifying for induction purposes. Registrants with unverified claims will be processed by the MEPS. A request for verification of prior-service or a copy of DD Form 214 will be prepared (via automated, telephonic, or manual methods) for registrants claiming prior-service if they are found otherwise qualified for induction. Such requests will contain the exact name under which the individual served, SSN, organization from which last discharged, and the type of discharge received. If exact dates of service are not known, approximate dates will be given. Requests will be submitted for the types of service and to the appropriate agency (figure 9–1). Recruiting services need to validate POCs/addresses.

Prior-service personnel who have been out of service at least nine months (unless indicated otherwise below) and have been completely discharged (that is, have no remaining Reserve obligation)	DIRECTOR NATIONAL PERSONNEL RECORDS CENTER (MILITARY PERSONNEL RECORDS) 1 RESERVE WAY ST. LOUIS, MO 63132-5200
Prior Marine Corps service personnel	COMMANDANT, US MARINE CORPS ATTN: MMSB WASHINGTON, DC 20380-1775
Prior Navy service personnel separated less than 9 months with or without Reserve obligation	CHIEF, BUREAU OF NAVAL PERSONNEL ATTN: PERS-312 MILLINGTON, TN 38054
Prior Coast Guard service personnel with Reserve obligation	U.S. COAST GUARD PERSONNEL COMMAND 4200 WILSON BLVD., SUITE 1100 ARLINGTON, VA 22203-1804
Prior Coast Guard service personnel separated less than 6 months without Reserve obligation	U.S. COAST GUARD PERSONNEL COMMAND 4200 WILSON BLVD., SUITE 1100 ARLINGTON, VA 22203-1804
Prior Coast Guard service personnel separated more than 6 months without Reserve obligation	DIRECTOR MILITARY PESONNEL RECORDS CENTER 1 RESERVE WAY ST. LOUIS, MO 63132
Prior Army service personnel separated less than 4 months with or without Reserve obligation-appropriate transfer point or separation activity	COMMANDER U.S. ARMY HUMAN RESOURCES COMMAND - ST. LOUIS ATTN: DARP-USE 1 RESERVE WAY ST LOUIS, MO 63132-5200
Prior Army service personnel separated more than 4 months with Reserve obligation	COMMANDER U.S. ARMY HUMAN RESOURCES COMMAND - ST. LOUIS ATTN: DARP-USE 1 RESERVE WAY ST LOUIS, MO 63132-5200
Prior ARNG service personnel with active duty and with or without Reserve obligation remaining, regardless of the time separated from active duty-adjutant general of the State from which member or former member was released to enter active duty.	ARMY NATIONAL GUARD READINESS CENTER ATTN: DIRECTOR OF PERSONNEL RECORDS 111 SOUTH GEORGE MASON DRIVE ARLINGTON, VA 22202
Prior Air Force service personnel with Reserve obligation, regardless of time separated	AIR RESERVE PERSONNEL CENTER ATTN: DPSPP DENVER, CO 80230, PHONE (303) 676-7071
Prior Air Force service personnel without Reserve obligation, regardless of time separated	MANAGER NATIONAL PERSONNEL RECORDS CENTER 1 RESERVE WAY ST LOUIS, MO 63132-5200

Figure 9–1. Points of contact for prior-service personnel

Table 9–1
Reenlistment eligibility codes not disqualifying for induction

Army	Marine Corps	Navy	Air Force	Coast Guard
RE–1	RE–1	RE–1	RE–1 with or	RE–1
RE–1A	RE–1A	RE–1E	without suffix	RE–1R
RE–1B	RE–3A	RE–1R		RE–3A (Note 3)
RE–2	RE–3E	RE–3B		RE–3B
RE–2A (Note 1)	RE–3F	RE–3D (Note 6)		RE–3C (Note 3)
RE–4A (Note 2)	RE–3H (Note 3)	RE–3E		RE–3D
	RE–3N	RE–3G		RE–3E
	RE–3O	RE–3H		RE–3F (Note 7)
	RE–3P (Note 4)	RE–3J		RE–3G
	RE–3R	RE–3K		RE–3K
	RE–3S (Note 5)	RE–3M		RE–3L
	RE–3T	RE–3N		RE–3M
	RE–3U	RE–3P (Note 4)		RE–3N
		RE–3Q		RE–P (Note 5)
		RE–3R		RE–3Q
		RE–3S (Note 5)		RE–3R
		RE–3T (Note 4)		RE–3S (Note 5)
		RE–3U		RE–3U
		RE–3X		RE–3X
		RE–3Y		
		RE–3Z		
		RE–5		
		RE–6		
		RE–7		

Notes:
[1] Grade determination will be processed by first duty station.
[2] Provided he meets citizenship requirements for induc ion as determined by the SSS.
[3] Provided he is not eligible for classification in Class 3–A (Registrant Deferred Because of Dependency on Others) as determined by the SSS.
[4] Provided he meets physical fitness standards for induction.
[5] Provided he is not eligible for classification in Class 4–G determined by the SSS.
[6] Provided he is not eligible for classification in Class 1–0 Alternative service) as determined by the SSS.
[7] Provided he meets maximum allowable weight standards for enlistment.

9–9. Conscientious objectors

Conscientious objectors will be classified Class 1–A–0 (Conscientious Objector Available for Noncombatant Military Service Only), and will be allocated as prescribed in this regulation. If the individual refuses, at any time, to be processed, the individual will be treated as an uncooperative registrant according to paragraph 9–11.

9–10. Registrants residing in foreign countries

The Director, Selective Service System, will establish procedures to process registrants living abroad as the situation warrants.

9–11. Uncooperative registrants

Registrants who are uncooperative will be withdrawn from the group. However, every effort will be made to complete the processing of these registrants. Registrants who refuse to take part in some or all of the required processing, testing, or examinations will be counseled as to the seriousness of their actions, and advised that persistence in such refusal constitutes a refusal to submit to induction which is a felony under Military Selective Service Act. The registrant will be informed that conviction of such an offense may result in the punishment of imprisonment for not more than five years or a fine of not more than $250,000 or both. If the registrant persists in refusing to take part in the required processing, the following action will be taken:

a. MEPS personnel who witness a refusal to be processed will prepare a signed, dated statement detailing the time, place, date, person, and circumstances involved in the refusal. The statement will be witnessed by at least two MEPS personnel who will authenticate the statement.

b. A letter of notification of refusal to cooperate will be prepared. The content and distribution of the letter will be as prescribed in figure 9–2 except that in lieu of reference to refusal to be inducted, a description of the facts concerning the registrant's refusal to cooperate will be included.

c. The registrant will be released from further processing.

d. The following is a sample of the letter of notification to be sent to U.S. Attorneys according to paragraph 9–41. It is not a standard format. Each MEPS may vary the content in accordance with instructions from the U.S. Attorney.

DEPARTMENT OF DEFENSE
HEADQUARTERS, UNITED STATES MILITARY ENTRANCE PROCESSING COMMAND
2834 GREEN BAY ROAD
NORTH CHICAGO, ILLINOIS 60064-3094

MCEA   May 12, 200X

SUBJECT: Refusal to Submit-to Induction

United States Attorney
US District Court
(Appropriate City and State)

Dear Sir:

In compliance with the provisions of Army Regulation 601-270, paragraph 9-40, the
following information is submitted pertaining to Mr. (Name), a Selective Service System
(SSS) registrant who refused to submit to induction on (Date) at the Military entrance
Processing Station, (Address of MEPS).
Full name and address of registrant: _____
_____. SSS Number: _____.
Number and address of SSS Local Board to which registrant is assigned: _____
_____. The name
of the registrant appearing on the SSS Delivery List, dated _____ indicating
the date of delivery as _____.* The registrant reported to the Military
Entrance Processing Station on   (Date) , and was processed for induction according to
applicable provisions of chapter 9 (Processing of Selective Service System Registrants) of
Army Regulation 601-270.

Mr. _____ was determined fully qualified for induction in all
aspects.

All registrants who were determined fully qualified for induction were assembled. The
Induction Officer informed them of the *imminence of induction*, quoting the following as
prescribed by Army Regulation 601-270, paragraph 9-39A.

*If the registrant was ordered to report to another MEPS, the date of the SSS delivery list
containing the subject registrant's name and reporting date is to be obtained through the *SSS
MLP* and cited in this letter. A statement will be added to reflect that the registrant was
ordered to report to one MEPS but reported to another and the reason therefore.

"You are about to be inducted into the Armed Forces of the United States, in the Army,
Navy, the Air Force, or the Marine Corps, as indicated by the Service announced following

Figure 9–2. Format of a letter to U.S. Attorney

CONTINUATION PAGE:

your name when called. You will take one step forward as your name and Service is called, and such step will constitute your induction into the Armed Forces indicated."
When Mr. _____'s name and service were called, he refused to step forward. He was removed from the presence of the group about to be inducted and processed as prescribed in Army Regulation 601-270, paragraph 9-40.

Mr. _____ persisted in refusing to submit to induction. He was informed that such refusal constitutes a felony under the provisions of the Military Selective Service Act of 1967, as amended. He was informed that conviction for such an offense under civil proceedings could subject him to punishment by imprisonment for not more than 5 years or a fine of not more than $25,000 or both. He was then informed again of the imminence of induction by the Induction Officer, who quoted the following: "You are about to be inducted into the Armed Forces of the United States, in the Army, Navy, the Air Force, or the Marine Corps, as indicated by the Service announced following your name when called. You will take one step forward as your name and Service is called, and such step will constitute your induction in the Armed Forces indicated."

Mr. _____'s name and Service were again called, but he still refused to step forward.

The above proceedings were witnessed by the following personnel:

WITNESSES:

(Complete names and addresses)

_____
_____
_____
_____
_____
_____

Attached is a statement prepared by _____
attesting to Mr. _____'s refusal to be inducted.

(Signature)

Copies furnished:

Region Manager, SSS

SSS MLP

MEPS FILE COPY

Figure 9–2. Format of a letter to U.S. Attorney—continued

9–12. Registrants of prominence

Registrants of prominence are individuals who by their personal ability in athletics, entertainment, business, Government, or other professions or activities are prominent members of their community. Additionally they may be members of families that are prominent in the area. These individuals will be processed as prescribed according to directions from Commander, USMEPCOM and the Director of the Selective Service System.

9–13. Processing of medical officers and other health specialists

The Health Care Personnel Delivery System (HCPDS) (DOD directive under development) provides procedures for registration and induction of physicians, dentists, nurses and other health care personnel in the event of a national emergency. The standby procedures would be implemented at the direction of Congress and may include entrance processing of both men and women at Military Entrance Processing Station (MEPS). The first health care registrants may report to MEPS as early as 90 days after the implementation decision.

9–14. Job reinstatement rights

Registrants will be advised of the following:

a. Federal law provides employment reinstatement rights to persons who leave positions (other than temporary) for the purpose of complying with the SSS induction notice and who are found not qualified for military service.

b. If registrants left their jobs for the purpose of being inducted and are found not qualified for military service, they should make application for their jobs at the next regularly scheduled work period following return to their residences. The law permits normal travel time from the MEPS to the person's residence.

c. If any difficulty is encountered in reclaiming a former job, communication should be made immediately with the nearest office of Veteran's Employment and Training Service, U.S. Department of Labor.

Section III
Determination of Moral Qualifications and Waivers

9–15. Initial screening

a. Individuals will be screened to ensure that only those qualified are processed for entry into the military services. Registrants are unacceptable when they have exhibited a record of convictions or other adverse adjudication (both adult and juvenile) reflecting frequent difficulties with law enforcement agencies, criminal tendencies, a history of anti-social behavior, alcoholism, other drug abuse, sexual misconduct, or questionable moral character. This will be accomplished by a Security Interview and ENTNAC.

b. Each registrant will be interviewed (either single or in a group) to determine if they meet the moral standards for induction. They will be asked if they have been convicted of any law violations by local, State or Federal authorities. This will include any and all traffic violations, and any adverse juvenile adjudication action. An example of each of the four categories in appendix F will be presented. They will also be asked if they are currently the subject of a criminal charge filed and pending against them by local, State or Federal authorities. Those who indicate a criminal law violation will complete a DA Form 4711 (Statement of Law Violations). See paragraph 9–15*d* below for further details. The DA Form 4711 will then be examined to determine if a waiver, as required by paragraph 9–18, is necessary.

c. An ENTNAC will be conducted on all inductees as outlined in paragraph 9–45.

d. Those registrants indicating past law violations will complete a DA Form 4711. It will be locally reproduced on 8 1/2 x 11-inch paper. The inductee will provide as complete a record as possible, detailing the exact circumstances of the violation(s), and final disposition of the charges. If the registrant meets the requisites for a waiver, the DA Form 2981 (Application for Determination of Moral Eligibility for Induction) will be completed. Applicants will be advised that these charges will be verified with the appropriate law enforcement agency.

9–16. Verification of self-admitted charges

Information furnished by judicial, police, and probation officials or other civil authorities (including character and employment references) will not be released to any person not having an official use for the information. All personnel will refrain from releasing the nature or source of any adverse information. When law enforcement or court officials refuse to release information concerning a registrant's offense record without their written consent, the registrant will be asked to provide written authorization. If verification cannot be obtained from other sources, the registrant's alleged record will be treated as unverified. Registrants will be advised at the time of the moral waiver interview that they can aid the reviewing authority in making a proper decision by providing a letter of character reference from reputable citizens. Further, registrants will be advised that the list of character references may be mailed (or hand-carried) to the MEPS if the references are properly identified and the list forwarded within the required time. Upon receipt of information from law enforcement agencies and/or courts, or probation or parole officials that they have no record of the alleged offenses, the notation "alleged offenses cannot be verified-no waiver required" will be recorded on DD

Form 1966 series. However, if the registrant alleges any offense that requires a waiver and the offense can be waived, a waiver will be initiated as an alleged offense.

a. Police checks. The MEPS will check with municipal, county, and State law enforcement agencies and appropriate courts, probation or parole officials, and correctional facilities to verify the disposition of adult felony offenses, alleged by the registrant or revealed by other reliable sources, and to determine the extent of rehabilitation. DD Form 369 (Police Record Check) will be used to make a check with law enforcement agencies. In states where records of offenses are centrally maintained, city and county police checks are not required, unless the registrant alleges recent conviction of an adult felony offense or that charges are pending. Otherwise, police checks will be made with municipal, county, and State law enforcement agencies in the following areas:

(1) Where the offense was alleged to have occurred.

(2) Where the registrant claimed residence and/or employment in the previous year.

(3) From other appropriate law enforcement agencies when receipt of a police check indicates that the case was handled by a different law enforcement agency.

b. Inquiries to courts. When there is an indication that charges against a registrant were disposed of judicially, an inquiry will be forwarded to the court concerned. In some jurisdictions, it may be possible to obtain this information from a probation or parole office or correctional institution instead of the court clerk. (For example, information concerning juvenile court records may be available only from juvenile probation or parole offices or correctional institutions.) In such cases, it is not necessary to send requests to both the court clerk and probation or parole officer.

c. Probation or parole officer's evaluations. In cases where police checks, the registrant, or other reliable sources indicate that the registrant was placed on probation or parole, an evaluation from the probation or parole officer should be obtained.

d. Correctional facility's evaluation. In the case of a registrant committed to a correctional facility (such as a reformatory, boys' school or ranch), a report will be requested from that facility.

e. Employer references. When the registrant indicates gainful employment (including part-time) in the previous year, the address of the employer will be requested to verify the employment and provide an evaluation of the registrant.

f. School evaluation. When the registrant attended school in the past 2 years, an evaluation from an official (such as a dean, principal, vice-principal, or counselor) or the last school the registrant attended will be requested when employer, probation, or parole evaluations are not available.

g. Offenses occurring in foreign countries. To the extent possible, efforts should be made to verify the disposition of charges which were actually or allegedly brought against the registrant by foreign countries. Registrants who are or allege they are subject to parole, probation, suspended sentence, or conditional release imposed by a foreign court will not be rendered unacceptable, and will be considered for waiver as though they were not subject to such civil restraint. Unverified offense records will be processed as outlined in h below.

h. Burden of proof. The burden of proof for registrant claims to bar induction such as unverifiable criminal offenses, and drug use, rests with the registrant. If the registrant does not have accompanying proof of the above claims, processing to determine overall qualification will be continued and, if otherwise qualified, the registrant will then be placed in the appropriate RBJ status. These registrants will be instructed to obtain documentation of their claims and bring them when they are recalled to the MEPS. These registrants will further be instructed that failure to provide documentation will invalidate their claims.

9–17. Preparation of DA Form 2981

Applications for moral waivers will be submitted on DA Form 2981 (Application for Determination of Moral Eligibility for Induction). The completion of all required items, as outlined below, is necessary to permit proper evaluation of the qualifications for military service of registrants.

a. Item 1. Include aliases (also known as). Also, include the date of birth.

b. Items 2 and 3. Self-explanatory.

c. Item 4. Include the actual name, instead of local abbreviations, of the offense as reported by supporting documents (police checks, court records, and so on), such as "assault with a deadly weapon" (not ADW) or "disorderly conduct" (not DC). A brief description of the offense will be included. When the offense is "contributing to the delinquency of a minor," the description will include the age of the minor as well as a brief narrative statement setting forth the nature of the delinquency. All offenses which resulted in convection or adverse juvenile adjudication will be entered in this section, including those which the registrant alleged but were not verified (para 9–16). Offenses reflected in police records may have been reduced or changed by the prosecutor or judge prior to or at the time of trial; hence, care must be taken to ensure that offenses entered are those for which the registrant was actually convicted or was subjected to an adverse juvenile adjudication by a court. Offenses will be listed in chronological order beginning with the earliest offense. The date of the offense and age of the registrant at the time of the offense will be stated. Offenses for which the registrant was not convicted or was not subject to an adverse juvenile adjudication will not be listed in this item.

d. Item 5a. Self-explanatory.

e. Item 5b. State the actual sentence handed down at the time of the disposition, followed by any amendments or changes which occurred later. If the disposition included probation or a suspended sentence still in effect, the conditions with which the defendant must comply will be stated (such as "cannot leave State," "report to probation officer weekly," "payment of a fine," or "sentence suspended during period of good behaviors"). If no conditions were imposed in conjunction with suspending the sentence or granting probation, and if the defendant was to be unsupervised, that will be stated. This information is necessary to enable approval authority to determine whether the probation or suspended sentence in effect comes within the definitions of "unconditional suspended sentence" or "unsupervised unconditional probation." Normally, accurate information concerning terms of probation or a suspended sentence is obtainable only from the court clerk or probation or parole authorities. Police records usually contain only an abbreviated entry, if any, concerning the disposition of charges, and seldom indicate the conditions of release upon conclusion of the trial. In referring to the offenses listed in item 4, DA Form 2981, correlate the date of the trial with the date of the offense. When making entries, include all information available.

f. Item 5c. Enter the maximum punishment which can be imposed for an adult under the State law for each offense listed in item 4, even though the defendant may have been handled by a juvenile court. If an offense is listed as a felony, for waiver purposes it will be processed as a felony, regardless of whether it is a felony or not in the State concerned. Likewise, if an offense is not listed as a felony for waiver purposes, but the offense is considered a felony by the local or State jurisdiction, it will be processed as a felony.

g. Item 5d. Enter the beginning and ending dates of confinement, parole, and/or probation. For moral waiver purposes, the term of "confinement" includes referral to or commitment in a facility for juveniles who have been subjected to an adverse juvenile adjudication, such as a juvenile camp, ranch, or home. The terms "probation" and "parole," include all types of official supervision imposed by courts and State agencies (such as correctional departments and State youth authorities). It may not be assumed that the individual was automatically released from civil restraint affective on the termination date of the probation or parole. Termination dates will be verified with the appropriate probation or parole authorities for all offenses listed in items 5a, b, and c.

h. Item 6. Indicate completion of school. (Show names of all employers, locations, inclusive dates (at least month and year), and job titles or brief descriptions, including part-time employment. Also, indicate periods of unemployment and a brief explanation of how the registrant subsisted while unemployed (such as "lived with parents").

i. Item 7. Block one will be checked when the registrant is interviewed by a moral waiver clerk at the MEPS. Block two will be checked when information is received by phone or personal interview with civil authorities. Block 3 will be checked only when the requests for information are completed and returned.

j. Item 8. Indicate the highest completed level of education. In those instances where 12 is listed as the highest education level of the registrant, indicate whether the registrant is a high school graduate, has a general education development (GED) certificate, or graduated from a special education institution.

k. Item 9. If only the AFQT portion was given, "NOT ADMINISTERED" will be entered in items 9a and b. If the registrant is determined qualified for induction under the provisions of paragraph 9–35, enter "ADMINISTRATIVELY ACCEPTED."

l. Item 10. Physical profile.

m. Item 11. Enter the AFQT composite percentile score.

n. Item 12.

(1) Describe any unsuccessful attempts to obtain offense verification or character references. Enter extenuating or mitigating circumstances concerning offenses listed in item 4 and any additional or clarifying information that should be considered in evaluating the waiver request. The following are examples of clarifying statements considered appropriate, if applicable. These are intended to illustrate only and are not intended as substitutes for statements of circumstances peculiar to each registrant.

(a) Registrant is a volunteer for induction. (If previous attempts to enlist were made, these will be summarized.)

(b) Registrant has requested reconsideration of a previously disapproved waiver. (Summarize any rationale provided by the registrant.)

(c) Registrant has voluntarily provided the attached additional information (cite) to support the waiver request.

(d) Registrant indicates that a poor environment, which has since improved, contributed to the actions. (Cite details, if available.)

(e) Registrant expressed deep regret for the past civil violations.

(f) Registrant stated that he wishes to improve his present situation.

(2) The following additional information is to be included, as appropriate.

(a) If there are more than two minor traffic offenses, indicate the number of offenses and location of information concerning them (such as "eight minor traffic offenses").

(b) Explain unusual acts which might indicate a questionable behavioral or character disorder.

(c) Express the apparent attitude or other demonstrable and significant observations about the registrant.

(d) Include an explanation of why certain police checks or court inquires are not present.

(e) Verbal verification of offenses or evaluations is of value if written information cannot be obtained. The statement "verbally from civil authorities," along with the name, title, and address of such authorities and the name and

title of the MEPS representative who obtained such information should be included in this item or in a separate written report signed by the MEPS representative who obtained it.

(f) List offenses for which the registrant was not convicted or subjected to an adverse juvenile adjudication and explain the disposition of each. Offenses to be listed here are those which were dropped, dismissed, or otherwise not prosecuted (nol prossed, nolle prosequi and nol pros); with or without leave; with or without prejudice; or in some similar way were removed from the category of a charge "pending." Accurate and complete information concerning these offenses will preclude the return of the case for further information concerning the disposition of the charges.

o. Item 13. Prior to making the appropriate recommendation, the station commander or his or her representative will determine whether the evidence being presented is sufficient to permit a proper evaluation by the Commander, USMEPCOM.

9–18. Waiver standards and approval authority

a. No waiver is required for the following:

(1) Five or fewer minor traffic violations in one year.

(2) One or two minor non-traffic offenses.

(3) One misdemeanor.

b. Registrants will be evaluated under the whole-person concept. Under this concept, a civil court record, combined with marginal aptitude and physical abilities, predicts marginal functioning. Such registrants may have difficulty adjusting to military stress and job performance demands. In addition to making a marginal contribution in the service, they often become disciplinary problems. Moral waivers will not be processed for registrants who are found otherwise not qualified for induction (such as failure to meet the minimum aptitude and/or medical standards). However, registrants found disqualified for induction due to temporary or remedial conditions will be processed for any required waiver of civil offenses. Registrants in the acceptability undetermined category (such as pending medical consultation or verification of prior-service) will also be processed for a waiver of any civil offense. Submission of the final request, however, will be held in abeyance until a final determination is made as to their aptitude and/or medical qualifications for service.

c. Waiver authority for all other offenses is listed in table 9–2. This authority is to both approve and deny the waiver in question.

d. Registrants who have criminal charges pending against them alleging violation of State, Federal, or territorial statute normally are unacceptable. Registrants, who have criminal charges pending against them alleging a violation of State, Federal, or territorial statute and as an alternative to trial for such violations, are granted a conditional release from the charge by a court on the condition that they will apply for induction into the military services, are also normally unacceptable. If a charge was dropped, dismissed, or not prosecuted (nol prossed, nolle prosequi, nol pros): "filed away"; with or without leave; with or without prejudice; or in some way removed from an active status; it is no longer pending. A charge is pending if the registrant is currently subject to "probation without verdict," "adjudication withheld and imposition of sentence suspended," or other similar deferral procedures. Registrants in this category will be processed to determine their overall qualification and, if otherwise qualified, will then be placed in the appropriate RBJ status. The MEPS will provide these registrants with a form that identifies the reason for their acceptability undetermined status so that if the registrant is recalled prior to final resolution of the case, the local SSS board can authorize an additional delay. Re-evaluation of moral qualification upon final disposition of criminal charges will be suggested to the SSS when registrants are found disqualified for induction on the basis of this paragraph. Similarly, re-evaluation of moral qualification upon final disposition of deportation proceedings will be suggested for aliens who have deportation proceedings filed and pending against them.

e. The provisions of *d* above do not apply to registrants who have charges pending against them involving minor traffic offenses. Registrants with such charges pending against them will be inducted, if otherwise qualified.

f. Registrants, who have pending against them a criminal charge of refusing to be inducted into the military services in violation of the Military Selective Service Act, may be processed for induction and inducted, if otherwise qualified, when the MEPS receives a letter (furnished directly to the MEPS or through the SSS area office) from the U.S. Attorney concerned with the prosecution of the registrant's case. The letter must reflect that—

(1) Neither the attorney nor the judge of the U.S. District Court concerned has any objection to the registrant's induction prior to judicial disposition of the charge.

(2) MEPS will give written notification to the appropriate U.S. Attorney following the induction of a registrant subsequent to the action prescribed in *d* above.

(3) Upon notification that the registrant has been inducted, appropriate action will be taken by the appropriate U.S. Attorney to accomplish dismissal of the charge against the person.

g. Registrants under parole, probation, suspended sentence, or conditional release from any terms of confinement are unacceptable, unless a waiver is obtained. Cases of unconditional suspended sentence or unsupervised unconditional probation will be considered for waiver at the appropriate level, depending on the nature of the offense. Cases of unconditional suspended sentence or unsupervised conditional probation for minor traffic offenses or less than three minor non traffic offenses require no waivers, providing the registrant has no record of additional convictions or adverse juvenile adjudications. The SSS area office is not required to obtain a release of registrants under unconditional probation prior to induction.

h. For consideration of a conditional waiver, the MEPS, in instances of registrants who have been ordered for induction and who are under parole, probation, suspended sentence or unsupervised unconditional release (other than unconditional suspended sentence or unsupervised unconditional probation), will request from the appropriate authorities all pertinent information concerning the case. MEPS commanders will forward cases involving felonies to the Commander, USMEPCOM for approval or disapproval of a waiver. MEPS commanders may process cases not involving felonies according to *a* above. Registrants for whom waivers are approved will be inducted, if otherwise qualified, upon receipt of information from the appropriate authorities that the registrant is released from all forms of civil restraint. It is not necessary that the person be released from that part of a court order requiring the person to provide support. (For example, in a paternity proceeding, the court may issue an order requiring support in addition to imposition of probation.) When the MEPS discovers that a registrant is subject to some form of conditional release, such as parole or supervised probation, the MEPS may process a waiver to determine acceptability for induction. Sample endorsements, to be used in connection with "conditional waiver" cases under this paragraph, are contained in figure 9–3.

i. For registrants under parole, probation, suspended sentence, or conditional release from any term of confinement imposed by a court for a violation of the Military Selective Service Act (on the condition that the registrant will report and submit to induction), the MEPS must request appropriate authorities to provide all pertinent information concerning the case for consideration of a conditional waiver (conditional upon obtaining the registrant's complete release from the charges and all forms of civil restraint prior to induction). (If the registrant refuses to provide a complete release, the registrant's alleged record will be treated as unverified. MEPS commanders will forward these cases through channels to the Commander, USMEPCOM for consideration of a waiver. Registrants for whom waivers are approved may be inducted, if otherwise qualified, after receipt of information that the registrant has been released from all forms of civil restraint. A sample endorsement, to be used by the Commander, USMEPCOM in connection with these "conditional waiver" cases, is contained in figure 9–3.

SAMPLE ENDORSEMENT FOR MORAL WAIVERS

The following endorsements to DA Form 2891 will be used for recording moral waiver determinations under the provisions of paragraph 9-18.

FILE _____ Ind
SUBJECT: Waiver of Civil Offenses

TO:

Request for waiver of civil offenses is approved and induction into the Military Services (Army, Navy, Marine Corps, Air Force or Coast Guard) is authorized, provided the registrant is otherwise qualified. This is not to be construed as authorization for induction into any Armed Force not currently accepting personnel for induction.

FOR THE COMMANDER:

_____

FILE _____ Ind
SUBJECT: Waiver of Civil Offenses

TO:

1. Request for waiver of civil offenses is approved and induction into the Military Services (Army, Navy, Marine Corps, Air Force or Coast Guard) is authorized, provided the registrant is otherwise qualified and a complete release from all forms of civil restraint, except for an unconditional unsupervised probation or unconditional suspended sentences has been obtained. This is not to be construed as authorization for induction into any Armed Force not currently accepting personnel for induction.

2. Upon receipt of information that the registrant is released from all forms of civil restraint or that the registrant is subject to only unconditional unsupervised probation or unconditional suspended sentences, the registrant may be inducted without further reference to a higher headquarters.

3. The registrant is (or it appears the registrant may still be) subjected to civil restraint as a result of the disposition(s) of offenses.

_____
_____
_____
_____

Figure 9–3. Sample endorsement for moral waivers

FOR THE COMMANDER:

_____

FILE _____Ind
SUBJECT: Waiver of Civil Offenses

TO:

1. Request for waiver of civil offenses is approved and induction into the Military Services (Army, Navy, Marine Corps, Air Force, or Coast Guard) is authorized, provided the registrant is otherwise qualified and a complete release from all forms of civil restraint (with the exception of registrants under unconditional unsupervised probation or unconditional suspended sentence), except the existing support court order has been obtained. This is not to be construed as authorization for induction into any Armed Force not currently accepting personnel for induction.

2. Upon receipt of information from the SSS area office that the registrant is released from all forms of civil restraint, except support court order, or that the registrant is subject to only unconditional unsupervised probation or unconditional suspended sentence, he may be inducted without further reference to a higher headquarters.

FOR THE COMMANDER:

_____

FILE _____Ind

SUBJECT: Waiver of Civil Offenses

TO:

Request for waiver of civil offenses for the purpose of induction into the Military Services (Army, Navy, Marine Corps, Air Force or Coast Guard) is not favorably considered.

FOR THE COMMANDER:

Note: Offenses are classified as a misdemeanor or felony per local and State Law.

Figure 9-3. Sample endorsement for moral waivers—continued

Table 9–2
Procedures for verifying offenses and processing moral waivers

Registrant states these law violations on DA Form 4711–R	Verification required?	Required verification documents	Prepared by:	After offenses verified, waiver is required	Waiver Authority
Minor traffic offenses 5 or less in 1 year	No				
Minor traffic offenses 6 or more in 1 year	Yes	DA 4711 DA 2981 DD 370	Registrant Registrant MW Clerk	Yes	MEPS CDR
Minor traffic offenses 2 or less	Yes	Same as above	Same as above	No	
Minor non-traffic offense 3 or more	Yes	Same as above	Same as above	Yes	MEPS CDR
1 misdemeanor	Yes	Same as above	Same as above	No	
2 or more non minor misdemeanors	Yes	Same as above	Same as above	Yes	MEPS CDR
Adverse juvenile adjudication for 1 or more juvenile "felonies"	Yes	Same as above	Same as above	Yes	See Note 1
1 adult felony	Yes	DA 4711 DA 2981 DD 370 DD 369	Registrant Registrant MW Clerk MW Clerk	Yes	USMEPCOM CDR
More than 1 adult felony	Yes	DA 4711 DA 2981	Registrant Registrant		Automatic Disqualify
Juvenile offenses with no convictions and no adverse adjudication	Yes	DA 4711	Registrant	No	
Alleged violations of State, Federal, and territorial statute with charges filed and pending	Yes	DA 4711 DA 2981 DD 370 DD 369	Registrant Registrant MW Clerk MW Clerk		See Note 2
Conditional release from criminal charges with induction into military service as alternative to trial	Yes	DA 4711 DA 2981 DD 370 DD 369	Registrant Registrant MW Clerk MW Clerk		See Note 3
Charges filed and pending for minor traffic offenses	No				

Notes:

[1] MEPS Commander may automatically disqualify without further review; or may forward documents to USMEPCOM for waiver.

[2] If alleged pending violations are verified, MEPS Commander must await final disposition of charges before determining whether waiver is required.

[3] MEPS Commander must await final disposition of charges. A registrant may not be inducted as an alternaive to trial.

9–19. Control of waiver documents

Moral waiver cases, while being processed, will be controlled. The proper file subdivision will be dictated by the volume of moral waivers being processed. When the reports essential to a valid determination are not returned within 30 days, the MEPS will contact the agencies concerned and request a prompt response. If the agencies fail to respond, the waiver will be forwarded for determination without the reports. When referred from law enforcement agency to another for verification of alleged offenses, MEPS commanders may exceed the 30 day period. Within 2 working days from receipt of the last report from school authorities, employers, police, court, probation or parole officials, or juvenile correctional facilities, the moral waiver will be submitted for determination.

9–20. Verbal waivers

Normally, moral waivers will be granted only on review of the written file by the approval authority. However, there may be instances when circumstances warrant telephonic requests and approval. The guides shown below will be used for verbal requests of induction moral waivers to the MEPS Commanders. USMEPCOM will determine whether a verbal waiver request for less than a felony offense must be processed in writing. Felony offense waivers must be initialed and approved or disapproved in writing and documented. Verbally approved waivers will be confirmed in writing (that is, the waiver file will be submitted to the approval authority for authentication). As a minimum the verbal request will confirm that—

    a. All known offenses for which the registrant was convicted or subjected to an adverse juvenile adjudication are described in the waiver request, including the date of the offense, date of trial, judicial disposition, inclusive dates of probation, confinement or parole.

    b. Police record checks have been made with the appropriate law enforcement agencies.

    c. The registrant is not known to be the subject of a pending charge other than minor traffic offenses or violation of the Military Selective Service Act.

    d. Efforts have been made to obtain reports from probation or parole officers and juvenile correctional facilities concerning the conduct of the registrant. Results of those efforts will be described in the waiver.

9–21. Deleted

Section IV
Medical Examination

9–22. Examination procedures
Medical examining policies, functions, and procedures are contained in chapter 8 of this regulation. Current medical fitness standards for induction are contained in DODI 6130.4. Testing for Human Immunodeficiency Virus (HIV) will continue during induction. Under the "One Step Process," the HIV test will be completed by the respective service during initial processing at the first training site. Under the "Two Step Process," HIV testing will be accomplished at the MEPS. Registrants will not depart until results of the test have been received. Drug and Alcohol Testing will be conducted in accordance with the approved mobilization guidance.

9–23. Disqualification for temporary conditions
When registrants are found disqualified due to temporary or remediable conditions, the reason will be recorded in DD Form 2808, item 73 (notes). It is the responsibility of the Chief Medical Officer to recommend to the MEPS Commander, when such an individual should be returned for a second examination.

9–24. Registrants claiming unverified ailments
SSS Form 233 (Order to Report For Armed Forces Examination) and SSS Form 252 (Order to Report for Induction) instructs registrants to bring a physician's statement or other evidence to substantiate any physical or aptitude ailment when reporting for induction processing. Disqualification of registrants solely on the basis of claimed but unverified ailments is not authorized. Registrants who claim disqualifying medical conditions but fail to bring substantiating documentation will be carefully evaluated, to include specialty consultation if appropriate. If practical, verification of ailments may be made telephonically by the MEPS medical officer, and the results recorded in item 73 (notes and/or continuation sheets of DD Form 2808). If written documentation substantiating the claimed ailments is considered necessary in order to render a fitness determination, the registrant will be asked to obtain the documentation and forward it within 2 weeks to the processing MEPS. Medical documentation received from private physicians, medical clinics, or other outside sources will be considered privileged information. Documents which are from doctors of medicine, osteopathy, dental surgery or other health care specialists and which indicate a record of past or current medical care will be attached to the DD Form 2808. The MEPS medical officer will indicate his or her review of the medical documents by making the following entry on the documents "Reviewed and considered in applicant's physical profile," and will date and initial the entries. A copy will be attached to each DD Form 2808 distributed at the time of enlistment and/or induction. The Chief Medical Officer determines the value of such documents in relationship to examination findings and to other pertinent medical information when determining the individual's medical qualification.

9–25. Registrants previously discharged for medical reasons
The medical reports (originals of DD Forms 2808 and 2807–1) pertaining to registrants who were previously discharged from the military service for medical reasons, and then found acceptable during induction processing, will be forwarded directly to the Chief, Enlistment Inquiry Section ATTN: TAPC–EPR–P Activity, 2461 Eisenhower Avenue, Alexandria, VA 22331–0450. SSS needs to validate this address. The Chief, Enlistment Eligibility Activity will secure and forward the current medical board reports, or other medical reports that caused the individuals separation from the last previous period of military service, to HQ USMEPCOM for determination of medical acceptability. When registrants are found disqualified, a notation of the reasons for medical disqualification will be entered in item 76 and 77 of all copies of DD Form 2808 (for example, "USMEPCOM Surgeon, 19 July 20XX, physically disqualified-rheumatic heart disease, ICD XXX.XX").

9–26. Registrants performing alternative service
The SSS may release registrants who are performing alternative civilian service if they become medically disqualified

for military service. Registrants in Class 1–W (Conscientious Objector Performing Alternative Service in Lieu of Induction) who claim disqualifying medical conditions will be scheduled for examination through coordination between the SSS MLP and MEPS. These registrants will be medically examined for the purpose of determining their acceptability under the standards prescribed for retention (AR 40–501, chapter 3 or other applicable service retention standards). Medical documentation received on the behalf of registrants will be carefully evaluated. Each document will be annotated to denote that it has been "reviewed and considered in the registrant's physical profile." A medical specialty consultation will be obtained when deemed appropriate. Costs incident to the medical examination and/or additional tests will be charged to USMEPCOM operating funds and paid on a non-reimbursable basis, unless reimbursement provisions are specified.

9–27. "Papers only" evaluation of registrants

SSS area offices may forward to the MEPS the documentation of the registrant's alleged medical condition. The documents will be reviewed to determine whether the claimed defects are obvious disqualifying conditions for military service. When a draft is instituted, USMEPCOM will distribute to SSS area offices an up-to-date listing of physical conditions considered as obvious disqualifications for military service when such list is provided by the Assistant Under Secretary of Defense (Health Affairs). A copy of the documents received from the SSS will be retained in the examination files. Originals will be returned to the SSS area office. The SSS will be advised of the determination rendered (either *a*, *b*, or *c* below).

a. If the condition is determined as an obvious disqualification: "Found not qualified for military service based on papers only evaluations."

b. If the condition is not determined to be an obvious disqualification: "The condition(s) described is/are not considered to be an obvious disqualification for military service. This is a papers only evaluation."

c. If a determination cannot be rendered: "The papers only documentation is not sufficient for the purpose of determining the registrant's qualifications for military service."

9–28. Medical disqualifications without a full examination

a. Registrants with clinically obvious demonstrable disqualifying conditions, such as marked shortening of a lower extremity with noticeable limp, or absence of an index, middle, or ring finger may be disqualified before the start of the examination. Additionally, registrants who present credible civilian medical documentation of a medical condition such as a history of asthma may also be disqualified without a medical examination.

b. When disqualified without a medical examination, the DD Form 2808, with identifying and administrative data filled in (items 1 through 16), will be annotated with details in item 77 and the disqualifying diagnoses in item 76. Copies of outside medical documentation will be attached to DD Form 2808. The MEPS physician will sign in item 84.

Section V
Testing

9–29. General testing procedures

The policies and procedures for test security, personnel facilities, equipment, administration, and scoring are contained in chapter 7. The purpose of administering the ASVAB to registrants is to—

a. Identify registrants who meet the standards for induction into the military services, and exclude those who fail to meet the established standards.

b. Provide the basis for qualitative distribution of inductees among the services currently accepting personnel for induction.

9–30. Terminal screening interviewers

Each MEPS will have one or more commissioned terminal screening interviewers assigned. Interviewers will conduct terminal screening of aptitude test failures according to paragraph 9–33. They will be assisted by enlisted psychology specialists, if available. The commissioned interviewers, however, will determine whether a registrant who failed to achieve qualifying test scores will be administratively accepted for military service.

9–31. Motivation of registrants

Before the ASVAB is administered, registrants will be informed that they should endeavor to do their best to achieve the highest possible scores, since these scores become a part of their permanent records, determine their eligibility for military service, and influence the type of training and jobs to which they will be assigned. Emphasis will be placed on the fact that a deliberate attempt to fail aptitude tests will not keep them out of the military service; they will be inducted (regardless of their score) if they are found not trying to do their best and otherwise could have passed. The duties of the test administrators and proctors include the detection of registrants who are not giving their full attention to the test. Whenever it is obvious that a registrant is not approaching the test in a proper manner after instruction and encouragement by the proctor, the examiner will withdraw the registrant from the testing session. The registrant will be referred to the terminal screening interviewer who will take one of the following actions:

a. If the commissioned officer determines that the registrant is incapable of understanding the test instructions, the commissioned officer will award the registrant a score of "0" on the AFQT composite of the ASVAB. Such registrants will be processed in the same manner as any other registrant who fails the AFQT. If such registrants are non-English-speaking, the following will be recorded on the ASVAB scoring worksheet: "AFQT–0 (non-English-speaking).

b. If the registrants marked answer sheets at random, refused to open test booklets, made no attempt to read or answer test questions, or took similar actions, an attempt will be made to obtain the registrant's cooperation. If the registrant agrees, the alternate test form will be administered. If the registrant again refuses to cooperate, the commissioned officer will recommend to the MEPS commander one of the following actions:

(1) That the registrant be administratively accepted according to paragraph 9–34.

(2) That the registrant be processed as an "uncooperative registrant" as prescribed by paragraph 9–11.

9–32. Induction standard

The induction standard is an AFQT score of 10 or above.

9–33. Retesting

Registrants who fail to attain qualifying aptitude test scores under the current induction standard may be retested if circumstances warrant. The MEPS commander is authorized to administer a retest, based upon supporting data such as high school or college transcript, job experience, and evidence of satisfactory completion of a Federal or State training program together with the terminal screening interview sheet. Provisions for the retesting of non-English-speaking registrants are contained in paragraph 9–34*c*(2)(*b*). Retesting of registrants who have attained qualifying scores for induction purposes while in an applicant status, or under the Armed Services Military Personnel Accession Testing Programs (AR 601–222), is not required if the scores are available at the MEPS.

9–34. Terminal screening

Administrative acceptance of registrants will be restricted to those registrants who are determined to have deliberately failed the tests and could have attained passing scores, under the current standards, had they been properly motivated. Registrants who have been malingering but considered unable to pass the tests will not be administratively accepted. The action is intended to ensure that only those registrants who can attain passing test scores under the current standards be inducted into the military services. Only devices authorized by HQDA will be used for terminal screenings. If earlier mobilization requirements dictate, however, an interim procedure is available at HQ USMEP-COM, ATTN: J–3/MOP, and will be implemented by separate instruction. A decision table for terminal screening and determining administrative acceptance is at figure 9–4.

a. Registrants failing to attain qualifying AFQT composite percentile scores. These registrants will receive final screening using the Deliberate Failure Keys (provided to MEPS by HQ USMEPCOM) and guidelines for the initial and final terminal screening interviews. Steps in the terminal screening procedures are as follows:

(1) Steps for non-high school diploma graduates.

(*a*) Those found by the Deliberate Failure Key to be in the True Failure Category or Undetermined Category will be rejected without additional terminal screenings

(*b*) Those found by the Deliberate Failure Keys to be in the Deliberate Failure category will be given an initial interview. The reason for the registrant's identification as a suspected deliberate failure will be explained and emphasis will be placed on increasing such a registrant's motivation to do better upon re-testing with an alternate form of the ASVAB.

(*c*) If a registrant suspected of deliberately failing refuses the opportunity to retest voluntarily, the initial interviewer will review all available information pertaining to the registrant's education and civilian occupation. Particular attention will be given to the registrant's educational level. Each registrant in this category who has ninth grade or lower as the registrant's highest educational level completed will be identified as a true failure and will not be screened further. All other registrants will be administered a final intensive interview by a commissioned officer. MEPS commanders or their designated representatives are authorized to correspond directly with either the registrant's school or employer to obtain school and job history records.

(*d*) When the evidence elicited in the final intensive interview clearly indicates that the registrant was poorly motivated in taking the test and would have achieved qualifying scores had the registrant tried to pass, the registrant will be administratively inducted as an AFQT Category IV.

(2) Steps for high school diploma graduates.

(*a*) These registrants will be screened with the Deliberate Failure Keys.

(*b*) If the terminal screening devices and final intensive interview by a commissioned officer reveal that the registrant had the aptitude ability to pass the AFQT portion of the ASVAB had he tried, the registrant will be administratively inducted as an AFQT Category IV. If, however, after the final, intensive, terminal screening interview, the interviewer believes that the failing AFQT composite percentile score of the registrant represents a true measure of the registrant's ability, the registrant will be rejected as not qualified for military service.

b. Registrants failing to attain qualifying scores. High school graduates and non-high school graduates failing to attain passing scores are not acceptable for induction unless found to be acceptable when terminally screened. The interviewer will review all available information pertaining to the registrant's education and civilian occupation. Particular attention will be given to the registrant's educational level. Each registrant who has ninth grade or lower as the registrant's highest educational level completed will be identified as a true failure and will not be screened further. All other registrants will be interviewed. When evidence elicited in the interview clearly indicates that the registrant was poorly motivated in taking the test and would have achieved qualifying scores had the registrant tried to pass, the registrant may be administratively accepted. If doubt exists as to whether or not the registrant should be administratively accepted, MEPS commanders or their designated representatives are authorized to correspond directly with either the registrant's school or employer to obtain school and job history records. Particular attention will be given to the General Technical composite (WK+AR+PC) score. If there is no conflict between the scores on the verbal and arithmetic reasoning tests (AFQT sub-tests) and the registrant's background, education, and job history, the registrant will not be administratively accepted. However, if there is a conflict, the registrant may be administratively accepted or a neuropsychiatry consultation may be obtained in doubtful cases.

c. Non-English-speaking registrants. Non-English-speaking registrants who failed to attain qualifying test scores will be processed as follows:

(1) Those found by the Failure Keys to be in the True Failure Category or Undetermined Category will be rejected without further processing.

(2) Those found by the Failure Keys to be in the Deliberate Failure Category and all high school graduates will be interviewed. Information from available personnel records pertinent to their English-speaking ability will be evaluated, and the registrants will be questioned on such matters as the length of time spent in this country, English-speaking opportunities or requirements at home or work, and the amount of English training they have had in school. With regard to these registrants, the interviewer will take the following actions:

(a) In those instances in which the interviewer suspects that a registrant is falsely claiming to be non-English-speaking or unable to read or write English, MEPS commanders or their designated representatives are authorized to correspond directly with either the registrant's school or employer to verify the interview findings. If the investigation indicates that the registrant was deliberately attempting to fail the tests and was fully capable of passing had the registrant tried, the registrant may be accepted. This decision, however, will be based on fully substantiated facts concerning the registrant's background. Registrants with academic training beyond high school or who hold professional jobs requiring use of the English language may be considered questionable cases. If there is evidence that the registrant was malingering, but the registrant's background does not indicate the aptitude ability to have passed, the registrant will be rejected.

(b) In those instances in which registrants are rejected solely because they are non-English-speaking, reexamination may be justified at a later date. Test scoring worksheets will be annotated "Non-English-speaking-RBJ after 6 months."

Table 9–3
Decision table for terminal screening and determining administrative acceptance

Education Level of Registrant and Failure Category	Screening Actions Required	Determination
1. Non-High School Graduates		
a. True failure as determined by failure keys		
	No further screening	Reject
b. Undetermined category as indicated by failure keys		
	No further screening	Reject
c. Deliberate failure as determined by failure keys	Terminal screening interviewers conduct initial/ intensive personal interviews	
(1) Mental ability to pass AFQT portion of ASVAB confirmed by screening devices and interview(s)	No further screening	Administratively accept
(2) Failing score determined by terminal screening interviewer to represent true measure of ability	No further screening	Reject
2. High School Graduates		
a. True failure	No further screening	Reject
b. Undetermined or del berate failure	Terminal screening interviewers conduct initial/ intensive personal interviews	
(1) See 1c(1)	See 1c(1)	See 1c(1)
(2) See 1c(2)	See 1c(2)	See 1c(2)
3. Non-High School Graduates/Non-English Speaking	No further screening	Reject
a. True failure		
b. Undetermined	No further screening	Reject
c. Failure with less than 12 months in CONUS	Annotate test scoring worksheet that reexamination may be justified later	RBJ for 6 months

Table 9–3
Decision table for terminal screening and determining administrative acceptance—Continued

d. Deliberate failure	Terminal screening interviewers conduct initial/ intensive personal interviews	
False claim to be non-English speaking suspected (malingering confirmed) but does not have mental capability to pass	No further screening	Reject

9–35. Terminal screening checklist
A checklist will be prepared for each registrant terminally screened. This checklist will include, but need not be limited to—

a. Name and SSN.

b. Test scores.

c. Deliberate failure key results.

d. Summary of the terminal screening interview, to include supplementary test scores and reasons for acceptance or nonacceptance.

e. Educational and job history background, to include copies of school records, if obtained.

Section VI
Induction Procedures

9–36. Orientation
Registrants found qualified for induction will be given orientations concerning the following:

a. The purpose and significance of induction.

b. The processing steps in which the registrant will participate, including the sequence and location of the processing.

9–37. Allocation of registrants
The allocation procedures prescribed in this paragraph will be invoked when more than one service is accepting inductees. Services accepting registrants will be constrained by a decentralized quality control program which ensures the service(s) receive the quality distribution needed to sustain the force. A cumulative report will be provided to each service, on a periodic basis, which reflects the distribution of the inductees apportioned to each service. This report will be sent to the headquarters of each recruiting service.

a. Determination of allocations. The five categories based on AFQT composite percentile scores are as follows:

(1) Category I: 93 to 99 AFQT percentile score.

(2) Category II: 65 to 92 AFQT percentile score.

(3) Category IIIA: 50 to 64 AFQT percentile score.

(4) Category IIIB: 31 to 49 AFQT percentile score.

(5) Category IV: 10 to 30 AFQT percentile score.

(6) Category V: 1 to 9 AFQT percentile score will not be used.

b. Application of allocation grouping system. Registrants are assigned to the services by predetermined allocation ratios. For example, if the allocation ratio for the Army was 50 percent then the Army would receive 50 percent of the registrants having a test rating of I. The allocation policy will conform to the registrant's preference of service. To indicate the registrant's preferences the following symbols will be used: Army-1, Navy-2, Air Force-3, Marine Corps-4, and None-N. These symbols will be added as the second factor to the basic allocation grouping system referred to in a above. For example, a registrant with a test rating of IV with no preference for service will have a basic group of IV–N. A registrant with a test rating of I with a preference for the Navy will have a basic grouping of I–2. As an exception, twins or other members of the same immediate family will be allocated to the same service if they so indicate a preference. Allocation of conscientious objectors will be no different than for other inductees, except as outlined in paragraph 9–37.

c. Allocation lists. Allocation lists will be prepared for each day on which inductions are to be accomplished. They will be prepared in the following manner:

(1) Separate lists will be prepared for the registrants in each test category group (that is, Category I-one list, Category II-one list, and so on). The heading of each list consist of the date of allocation and test category group. The names on each list will be arranged in alphabetical order. After each name, the registrant's service preference will be indicated.

(2) Tentative allocations will be made on the basis of each registrant's service preference. Totals of the tentative allocations will be indicated as shown in figure 9–4.

(3) Totals of the tentative allocations will be compared with the authorized ratios to determine the degree of adjustment necessary in each service allocations.

(4) If, following tentative allocations, a shortage exists in any service allocation and there are registrants who have not expressed a service preference, these registrants will be assigned to the service in which the shortage exists. Such registrants must be assigned prior to changing the allocation of any registrant who has expressed a service preference.

(5) If there is need for further readjustment between the tentative allocations and required ratios, the following action will be taken:

(a) In the Armed Forces (Army, Navy, Air Force, or Marine Corps) having an excess in the tentative allocation, begin at the top of the alphabetical list and select each fourth registrant for final allocation to the service having a shortage. So far as possible, every fourth registrant will be assigned in conformance with his second service preference.

(b) For further adjustments, the above process of selection will be reversed by starting at the bottom of the list until the allocations fall within the prescribed ratios.

d. Cumulative allocation adjustment. Since only fractional shortages or an excess of allocation ratios are permissible, the daily allocation list cannot always conform to the required ratios. Fractional differences, however, can be adjusted on subsequent allocations. To accomplish such adjustments, cumulative records of allocations will be maintained and, by continuous adjustments of the daily allocation to required ratios, the final monthly totals of allocations to the four services can be accomplished within the authorized ratios.

e. Automated allocations. Automated allocations may be utilized in lieu of the manual allocation procedures outlined in paragraphs 9–37a through *d* above. Note: Enter service preference in this column using code designation as follows: Army-1, Navy-2, Air Force-3, Marine-4, none-N For purposes of illustration only. In the event of mobilization, the actual distribution table will be provided by OSD in coordination with services. In the event of mobilization, the actual distribution will be provided by OUSD (P&R) in coordination with the services.

Category A-1

Allocation to: _____

Trainee	pl	Army(1) Tentative	Army(1) Final	Navy(2) Tentative	Navy(2) Final	Air Force(3) Tentative	Air Force(3) Final	Marine Corps(4) Tentative	Marine Corps(4) Final
Allen, Henry...	13	X	X						
Bingham, Charles	21			X	X				
Dahon, John	23			X	X				
Eriss, Wilson	31					X	X		
Evans, Walter	12	X	X						
Laury, Winston	32					X	X		
Lewis, George	43							X	X
Moser, John	12	X	X						
Munson, John	12	X	X						
Munson, Reginald	31					X	X		
Nune, Paul	13	X	X						
Paterson, David	12	X	X						
Peterson, Wylie	N	X	X						
Post, James	23			X					
Runner, William	23			X	X				
Russell, Frank	21			X	X				
Russell, William	21			X	X				
Stone, Paul	13	X	X						
Thomas, William	12	X	X						
Williams, Fred	32					X	X		
Total		9		6		4		1	
Tentative		9							
Authorized				5		4		1	
Quota		10							
Final						4			
Total		10		5				1	

Computation of authorization: Total listed 20

.50	10 Army
.25	5 Navy
.20	4 Air Force
.05	1 Marine Corps

Figure 9–4. Allocation record

9–38. Conscientious objectors allocated to the Marine Corps

The Military Selective Service Act prescribes that inductees classified as conscientious objectors (1–A–0) by the SSS will be assigned to noncombatant service. Noncombatant service, as defined in paragraph 9–8, will be explained to registrants who have through allocation procedures, been assigned (for induction purposes) to the Marine Corps. They will then be afforded the opportunity to declare whether or not the occupational fields available in the Marine Corps are acceptable to them. DA Form 3544 (Statement of Understanding-Conscientious Objectors (1–A–0)) will be used for this purpose. Those who desire further counseling concerning their rights and opportunities available in the Marine Corps will be referred to the Marine Corps liaison representative. Registrants who decline assignment to all of the noncombatant occupational fields available in the Marine Corps will be inducted into other military services currently accepting inductees (of the individual's preference, if possible) where medical occupational specialty assignments are available. Cumulative records of allocations maintained according to paragraph 9–37d will be adjusted accordingly. The completed statement will be forwarded with other records to the appropriate Marine Corps recruit depot or filed with a copy of the allocation list, depending upon whether the individual accepts or declines assignment to the occupational fields available in the Marine Corps.

9–39. Induction

The following procedure will be followed in the induction of all registrants into the military services:

a. Registrants who have been determined to be fully qualified for induction in all respects will be assembled. The induction officer will inform them of the imminence of induction quoting the following:

"You are about to be inducted into the Armed Forces of the United States, in the Army, the Navy, the Air Force, or the Marine Corps, as indicated by the service announced following your name when called. You will take one step forward as your name and service are called and such step will constitute your induction into the Armed Forces indicated."

b. Registrants who fail or refuse to step forward when their name is called will be removed quietly and courteously from the presence of the group about to be inducted and processed (see para 9–40).

c. A commissioned officer or warrant officer (see para 6–7a) then will call the roll and the foregoing procedure will be carried out. All who have stepped forward will be informed that each and every one of them is a member of the military services concerned, using the language exactly as stated:

"You have now been inducted into the military services of the United States indicated when your name was called. Each one of you is now a member of the military services concerned, and amenable to regulations and the Uniform Code of Military Justice and all other applicable Laws and regulations."

9–40. Oath of allegiance ceremony

The oath of allegiance is not a part of the induction. Registrants who have been inducted will be informed that the taking of the ceremonial oath of allegiance is not part of the induction. The oath will be administered by any commissioned officer of any military service as soon after the induction. In every instance, there will be an appreciable break to ensure that the taking of the ceremonial oath does not appear to be any part of the induction. MEPS commanders may permit the oath to be administered at other locations if requested by the service in which inductee was inducted. Inductees will be informed of their right to take the oath of allegiance by affirmation and to omit "So help me God." If a non-declared alien is a member of the newly inducted group, the officer will explain the difference between the ceremonial oath of allegiance and the ceremonial oath of service and obedience.

a. The oath of allegiance reads as follows:

"I (name), do solemnly swear (or affirm) that I will support and defend the Constitution of the United States against all enemies, foreign and domestic; and I will bear true faith and allegiance to the same; and that I will obey the orders of the President of the United States and the orders of the officers appointed over me, according to regulations and the Uniform Code of Military Justice. So help me God."

b. In the event of non-declarant aliens not desiring to take the oath of allegiance, they may be administered the following oath of service and obedience:

"I (name), a citizen of (country of citizenship) and without intention of surrendering such citizenship, do solemnly swear (or affirm) that I will serve the United States honestly and faithfully against all their enemies whomsoever, and that I will obey the orders of the President of the United States and the orders of the officers appointed over me, according to regulations and the Uniform Code of Military Justice."

c. Inductees who refuse to subscribe to the oath of allegiance or oath of service and obedience, whichever is appropriate, will be advised that they are already members of the United States Army, Navy, Air Force, or Marine corps, whichever is appropriate.

d. Immediately following the induction and oath of allegiance or oath of service and obedience, Art 85 (Desertion) and Art 86 (Absent without leave) of the UCMJ, will be explained to all inductees. Inductees will also be advised that they are subject to the UCMJ and that the required articles will be explained to them within a few days after arrival at their first duty station.

9–41. Refusal to submit to induction

Registrants who have been removed from the group as prescribed in paragraph 9–38*b* and persist in their refusal to submit to induction will be informed that refusal constitutes a felony under the provisions of the military Selective Service Act, 50 USC 462. They will be further informed that conviction of such an offense under civil proceedings will subject them to punishment by imprisonment for not more than 5 years or a fine of not more than $250,000, or both. They will then be informed again of the imminence of induction using the language specified in paragraph 9–38*a*, and their names and services again will be called. If they step forward at this time, they will be informed that they are a member of the military services concerned, using the language specified in paragraph 9–38*c*. If, however, they persist in refusing to be inducted, the following action will be taken:

a. Registrants who refuse induction will not be furnished any means of transportation.

b. A letter of notification of refusal to submit to induction will be prepared in three copies. (See fig 9–3 for a sample format.) The original, together with the statement described in paragraph 9–10*a*, will be submitted to the US Attorney for the judicial district in which the MEPS is located. One copy will be forwarded to the SSS MLP and one copy will be retained at the MEPS. USMEPCOM will also update the registrant's status in the data base. Notification will include the following information:

(1) Name, SSN and address of registrant and witnesses.

(2) Registrant's SSN.

(3) Address of SSS area office.

9–42. Name in which inducted

Ordinarily, a registrant will be inducted into the military services in the name which appears on the Order to Report for Induction. However there is no regulatory or statutory requirement that a registrant be inducted only in the name reflected on the induction order or other records and forms accomplished by the SSS, birth certificate, baptismal certificate, or court order authorizing change of name. In the absence of evidence of fraudulent intent (for example, to evade law enforcement officials or to conceal a criminal record), there is no legal objection to the induction of a registrant in the name he has assumed and later claims at the time of induction. The registrant's assumed name will be placed on DD Form 1966 series, and other records prepared during the induction processing. The previous name will be noted on those records. The disposition reported to the SSS will be in the enlistment packet.

9–43. Grade in which inducted

All registrants inducted under this regulation will be inducted in grade E1. Registrants may be inducted in the grade of E2, who have completed any of the following: 3 or 4 years of Junior Reserve Officers Training Corps (JROTC) Program (or the equivalent National Defense Cadet Corps program) or 2 or more years of college level Reserve Officers Training Corps. Documentation reflecting the successful completion is required. Those individuals who lack documentation will be inducted in grade E1; however, they may present documentation to their personnel officer at any time prior to the completion of 4 months of service and request appropriate grade adjustment. The effective date of grade, for rank and pay purposes, will be adjusted to the date of induction upon the presentation of documentation to the personnel officer. USMEPCOM will receive guidance from OSD regarding which grade to induct health care professionals.

9–44. Personnel affairs orientation

Inductees will be given orientations concerning their rights under the service members Civil Relief Act and legal assistance, regarding the advisability of having a will, powers of attorney, and estate planning, while on AD. General leave policies (provisions for 30 days of annual leave and respective service procedures for granting leave upon completion of basic or advanced training) will also be explained.

9–45. Entrance national agency check/national agency check

ENTNACs are required by Department of Defense Regulation 5200.2R on all inductees.

a. Services will have the responsibility to prepare and submit the SF86/Electronic Personnel Security Questionnaire to the appropriate agency and provide a copy to the MEPS.

b. MEPS will have the responsibility to—

(1) Print and submit the FD 258 (fingerprint card) or transmit the electronic fingerprint file.

(2) Forward, by the end of each workday, FD 258 to the appropriate background investigation agency, if fingerprints cannot be processed electronically.

c. If the induction process is in the "One Step" mode, results of the ENTNAC will be forwarded by USMEPCOM to the service. Service Commanders will investigate and determine whether or not the service member should be retained based on their moral qualifications.

d. If the induction process is in the "Two Step" mode, USMEPCOM will forward results to the services for any inductees who have already departed, USMEPCOM will process moral waivers on information revealed from an ENTNAC on inductees who have not departed.

Section VII
Preparation and Disposition of Records and Disposition Reporting

9–46. Induction travel orders

Orders will be prepared to direct the travel of inductees. See figure 9–5 for a sample of induction travel orders.

HEADQUARTERS, UNITED STATES MILITARY ENTRANCE PROCESSING COMMAND
2834 GREEN BAY ROAD
NORTH CHICAGO, ILLINOIS 60064-3094

MCEA   May 12, 200X

Induction Travel Order No. 111-11

1. Having been inducted into the United States Army this date, in pay grade E1, unless
other wise indicated, the following personnel are assigned and will report to FORT KNOX,
KENTUCKY no later than 12:00 PM (midnight), 10 July 20___, unless otherwise indicated
below.
Remarks/

2. NAME/SSN Special Instructions -

*DOE, JOHN J. 111-11-1111

JOHNSON, GARY W. 222-22-2222   Inducted in pay grade E3

SMITH, PETER E. 333-33-3333
JONES, EDWARD S. 444-44-4444

                                /s/ Allen S. Craig, CPT, USAF
DISTRIBUTION: /t/   PETER S. JOHNSON
1-ea inductee   Major, USA
2-group leader
3-Ft. Knox, KY

                          * Group leader 2

Figure 9–5. Sample induction travel order

9–47. Disposition of induction records

a. The following documents will be forwarded to the initial reception activity:
(1) Induction travel orders (three copies).
(2) DD Form 2808, originals and any supporting documents.
(3) DD Form 2807–1, originals.
(4) DA Form 4711, original (when applicable), and DA Form 2981.
b. One copy of the induction travel order document will be furnished to the inductee.
c. The following documents will be retained at the MEPS:
(1) For inductees, the following documents will be retained at the MEPS for 3 months and then destroyed.
(a) DD Form 2808, one copy, including supporting documents (when applicable).

(b) DD Form 2807–1, one copy.

(c) Waiver of civil offenses, one copy (when applicable).

(d) ASVAB score records.

(2) For registrants who are found disqualified for service (including those found disqualified due to temporary or remedial conditions), the ASVAB score records will be retained at the MEPS for 2 years and then destroyed. The following documents will be retained at the MEPS for 1 year and then destroyed.

(a) DD Form 2808, one copy, including supporting documents (when applicable).

(b) DD Form 2807–1, one copy.

(c) DA Form 4711, original (when applicable).

(d) DA Form 2981.

9–48. Registrant processing disposition

Upon completion of the processing procedures set forth in this chapter, USMEPCOM will report accession information to the SSS and the services concerned and report registrant examination information to the SSS. USMEPCOM will report dispositions by the means and in the manner specified and agreed upon in Memorandums of Understanding.

9–49. The Health Care Personnel Delivery System

The Health Care Personnel Delivery System (HCPDS) provides procedures for registration and induction of physicians, dentists, nurses and other health care personnel in the event of a national emergency. The standby procedures would be implemented at the direction of Congress and may include entrance processing of both men and women at a Military Entrance Processing Station (MEPS). The first health care registrants may report to MEPS as early as 90 days after the implementation decision.

Appendix A
References

Section I
Required Publications

AR 25–30
The Army Publishing Program (Cited in para 3–13 and 5–1*c*.)

AR 40–501
Standards of Medical Fitness (Cited in paras 8–2*b*(1), 9–26, appendix F–4.)

AFI 48–123
Medial Examination and Standards (This publication is available from the Air Force Publication Distribution Office, 4008A, Bolling Air Force Base, Washington, D.C. 20332 or at http://www.e-publishing.af.mil/?txtSearchWord=AFI48-123v1&rdoFormPub=rdoPub.) (Cited in para 8–2*b*(3).)

AR 601–222/OPNACINST 130.1A/MCO 1130.52F/AFJI 36–2016/CG COMDINST 1130.52B
Armed Services Military Personnel Accession Testing Programs (Cited in paras 2–1*l*(5), 2–2*p*, 3–2*a*(1), 7–1*a*, 7–5*a*, 9–33.)

DTR 4500.9–R
Defense Travel Regulation (Cited in para 6–9.)

Section II
Related Publications
A related publication is a source of additional information. The user does not have to read it to understand this publication. U.S. Code is available at www.gpoaccess.gov/uscode.

AR 12–1
Security Assistance, Training, and Export Policy

AR 20–1
Inspector General Activities and Procedures

AR 25–400–2
The Army Records Information Management System (ARIMS)

AR 135–100
Appointment of Commissioned and Warrant Officers of the Army

AR 135–101
Appointment of Reserve Commissioned Officers for Assignment to Army Medical Department Branches

AR 380–67
Department of the Army Personnel Security Program

AR 601–210
Active and Reserve Components Enlistment Program

AR 601–222
Armed Services Military Personnel Accession Testing Programs

DODD 1145.02E
United States Military Entrance Processing Command (Available at www.dtic.mil/whs/directives.)

DODD 1315.07
Military Personnel Assignments (Available at www.dtic mil/whs/directives.)

DODD 6130.3 (delete – erroneously listed)
Medical Standards For Appointment, Enlistment, or Induction in the Armed Forces (Available at www.dtic.mil/whs/directives.)

DODI 1304.8
Military Personnel Procurement Resources Report (Available at www.dtic.mil/whs/directives.)

DODI 4000.19
Interservice and Intragovernmental Support (Available at www.dtic.mil/whs/directives.)

DODI 6130.03 (corrected title)
Medical Standards for Appointment, Enlistment, or Induction in the Armed Forces (Available at www.dtic.mil/whs/directives.)

NAVMED P–117
Manual of the Medical Department (MANMED) (Available at http://med.navy mil/pages/default.aspx)

NAVMILPERSMAN/NAVPERS 15560
Navy Military Personnel Manual (This publication is available from Navy Publications and Forms Center, 5801 Tabor Avenue, Philadelphia, PA 19120 SN 0500–LP–277–8290.

ANGI 36–2005
Appointment of Officers in the Air National Guard of the United States and as a Reserves of the Air Force (Available at http://www.e-publishing.af mil.)

NGR 600–200
Enlisted Personnel Management (Available at http://www.ngbpdc ngb.army.mil/pubs.)

UCMJ
Uniform Code of Military Justice (Available at http://www.ucmj.us.)

USMEPCOM Reg 20–1
Inspector General Inspection Program (Available at http://www mepcom.army mil/publications/index html)

5 USC 552a
Records maintained on individuals

10 USC 502
Enlistment oath: who may administer

Section III
Prescribed Forms
Unless otherwise indicated, DA forms are available on the APD Web site (www.apd.army mil).

DA Form 2981
Application for Determination of Moral Eligibility for Induction (Cited in paras 9–15, 9–17, 9–47.)

DA Form 3544 (canceled but cited in publication)
Statement of Understanding-Conscientious Objectors (Cited in para para 9–38.)

DA Form 4711
Statement of Law Violations (Cited in paras 9–15, 9–47, table 9–2.)

Section IV
Referenced Forms
Unless otherwise indicated, DD forms are available on the OSD Web site (www.dtic.mil/whs/directives/infomgt/forms/formsprogram htm); Standard Forms (SF) and Optional Forms (OF) are available on the GSA Web site (www.gsa.gov).

DA Form 1811 (canceled but cited in publication)
Physical Data and Aptitude Test Scores Upon Release from Active Duty

DD Form 4 (deleted the word Series)
Enlistment/Reenlistment Document - Armed Forces of the United States

DD Form 93
Record of Emergency Data

DD Form 214
Certificate of Release or Discharge from Active Duty

DD Form 215
Correction to DD 214, Certificate of Release or Discharge from Active Duty

DD Form 368 (corrected title)
Request for Conditional Release from Reserve or Guard Component (EGA)

DD Form 369
Police Record Check

DD Form 1966 (deleted the word Series)
Record of Military Processing Armed Forces of the United States

DD Form 2807–1
Report of Medical History

DD Form 2807–2
Medical Prescreen of Medical History Report

DD Form 2808
Report of Medical Examination

NGB Form 22
Report of Separation and Record Service (Available at www.ngbpdc.ngb.army.mil.)

SF 86
Questionnaire for National Security Positions

SF 1034
Public Voucher for Purchases and Services Other than Personal

SSS Form 233
Order to Report for Armed Forces Examination

SSS Form 252
Order to Report for Induction

USMEPCOM Form 680–3A–E
Request for Examination (Available at www.mepcom.army.mil.)

USMEPCOM Form 727–E
Processing List (Available at www.mepcom.army.mil.)

USMEPCOM Form 37–1–2–R–E
Itemized Listing of Medical Services for Medical Examinations Public Vouchers (Available at www.mepcom.army. mil.)

Appendix B
Standards for MEPS Ceremonial Rooms

AR 601–270/OPNAVINST 1100.4C CH–1/MCO 1100.75F/COMDTINST M 1100.2E
23 March 2007/RAR 13 September 2011

B–1. Ceremonial room decor and equipage

a. Ceremonial room decor and equipage will be as specified by USMEPCOM Regulation 420–3–3.

b. Rostrum of professional quality with DOD seal affixed.

c. Flag, National, United States, 4'4" hoist by 5'6" fly, nylon or silk.

d. Flag, State, to represent each state served by the MEPS and will be displayed by the date the State joined the Union.

e. Flag, organization, U.S. Army, U.S. Marine Corps, U.S. Navy, U.S. Air Force and U.S. Coast Guard.

f. Seals, U.S. Army, U.S. Marine Corps, U.S. Navy U.S. Air Force, and U.S. Coast Guard.

B–2. Ceremonial rooms

Ceremonial rooms will be used only for administering the Oath of Enlistment, Oath of Service and Obedience, and other auspicious events such as change of command, presentation of awards, and other ceremonies.

Appendix C
Special Purpose Test

C–1. Authorized Test

Special purpose tests are administered to personnel who are eligible for applicable tests when sponsored by the appropriate service commander or representative. These requests require local level advanced coordination.

C–2. Special Test

The following tests are authorized to be given in the MEPS.

a. Air Force Officer Qualifying Test (Air Force only).

b. American Language Course Placement Test (ALCPT).

c. Auditory Perception Test (Army, Air Force, and Marine Corps. May be referred to as Army Radio Code Test (ARC)).

d. Defense Language Aptitude Battery (Army, Navy, Air Force, and Marine Corps only).

e. Defense Language Proficiency Test (Army, Navy, Air Force, and Marine Corps only).

f. Electronic Data Processing Test (Marine Corps and Air Force only).

g. English Comprehension Level Test (Available for use by Army, Air Force, and Marine Corps).

h. Alternate Flight Aptitude Selection Test (Army only).

i. Assessment of Individual Motivation (Army only).

j. Basic Attribute Test (BAT) (Air Force only).

k. Coding Speed (CS) Navy only).

l. Spanish Wonderlic Personnel Test (SWPT) (Army only).

Appendix D
Assignment Qualifications

D–1. Officer assignment qualifications

The following table below (table D–1) lists the assignment qualifications for officers.

Table D–1
Assignment qualifications for officers

PRIVATE Position	Grade	Qualifica ions	Asgmt Overlap	Tour Length
HQ/Sector Staff	02/06	Determined by proponent service	Contact	3 years
Sector Cdrs.	06	Determined by proponent service	2 weeks	2 yrs w/3d yr coordinated on case-by-case basis.

Table D–1
Assignment qualifications for officers—Continued

PRIVATE Position	Grade	Qualifications	Asgmt Overlap	Tour Length
MEPS Cdrs. Baltimore Chicago Dallas Los Angeles New York Montgomery	05	CGSC/AFSC grad or equivalent.	2 weeks	3 years
MEPS Cdrs. All others	04	CGSC/AFSC grad or equivalent. XO screened or grad of Amphib. Warfare School or equivalent intermediate school. Successful company command.	Contact	3 years
MEPS Operations Officer	03/04	Advanced course grad or equivalent.	Contact	3 years

D–2. Enlisted assignment qualifications

a. Assignment qualifications. Enlisted personnel selected for assignment to USMEPCOM must be mature individuals with sufficient military experience and personal stability to perform independently with a minimum of supervision and leadership. The following criteria are essential in identifying individuals professionally qualified and personally prepared for assignment to HQ USMEPCOM. While career enhancing, the enlisted tour length in USMEPCOM is limited to 36 months or Navy personnel shore tour length not to exceed 48 months. This rotation schedule allows for professional development.

b. Minimum grade. E–5. Enlisted personnel below the grade of E–5 will not be assigned to a MEPS without approval of the Commander, USMEPCOM.

c. Time in service. 3 years. Personnel with less than 3 years of active service will not be assigned without the approval of the Commander, USMEPCOM.

d. Retention. Minimum of 3 years of service to expiration of term of service (ETS) after arrival at the MEPS.

e. Education. High school graduate.

f. Communication skills. Read and speak English clearly. The daily conduct of group briefings and individual instructions to applicants requires all assigned personnel meet this qualification. Non-DOD documents supporting applicant processing demand understanding to determine required action.

g. Financial stability. Have demonstrated financial responsibility. Additional expense of living in a civilian community must be expected. Support facilities and activities normally associated with a major military installation may not be available.

h. Personal character. No record of convictions by courts-martial or civil authority. An individual with an identified drug or alcohol problem will not be assigned to a MEPS. No record of non-judicial punishment under UCMJ, within the last 3 years.

i. Driver's license. No physical limitations preventing the operation of a military sedan.

j. Appearance. Meet height/weight and grooming standards of their service.

Appendix E
Guidelines of Typical Offenses

E–1. Minor traffic offenses

Offenses of a similar nature and traffic offenses treated as minor by local law enforcement agencies should be treated as minor by the military. The following list is intended as a guide:

- Blocking or retarding traffic.
- Careless driving.
- Crossing yellow line; driving left of center, disobeying traffic lights, signs, or signals.
- Driving on shoulder.
- Driving uninsured vehicle.
- Driving with blocked vision.
- Driving with expired plates or without plates.

- Driving without license or with suspended or revoked license.
- Driving without registration or with improper registration.
- Driving wrong way on one-way street.
- Failure to comply with officer's directives.
- Failure to have vehicle under control.
- Failure to keep to right or in line.
- Failure to signal.
- Failure to stop for or yield to pedestrian.
- Failure to submit report following accident.
- Failure to yield right of way.
- Faulty equipment: defective exhausts horn, lights, mirror, muffler, signal device, steering device, tailpipe, windshield wipers.
- Following too closely.
- Improper backing: backing into intersection or highway, backing on expressway, backing over crosswalk.
- Improper blowing of horn.
- Improper parking: restricted area, fire hydrant, double parking.
- Improper passing: passing on right, in no-passing zone, passing parked school bus, pedestrian in crosswalk.
- Improper turn.
- Invalid or unofficial inspection sticker; failure to display inspection sticker.
- Leaving key in ignition.
- License plates improperly displayed or not displayed.
- operating overloaded vehicle.
- Racing; dragging; contest for speed.
- Reckless driving (single offense).
- Speeding.
- Spinning wheels; improper start; zigzagging or weaving in traffic.

E–2. Minor non-traffic offenses

Offenses of a similar nature should be treated as minor offenses. In doubtful cases, the following rule should be applied: if the maximum confinement under local law is 4 months or less, the offense should be treated as minor. The following list is intended as a guide:

- Abusive language under circumstances to provoke breach of peace.
- Carrying concealed weapon (other than firearm); possession of brass knuckles.
- Curfew violation.
- Damaging road signs.
- Discharging firearm through carelessness.
- Discharging firearm within municipal limit.
- Disobeying summons.
- Disorderly conduct; creating disturbance; boisterous conduct Disturbing the peace.
- Drinking liquor on train (other than club car).
- Drunk in public; drunk and disorderly.
- Dumping refuse near highway.
- Fighting; participating in affray.
- Fornication.
- Illegal betting or gambling; operating illegal handbook, raffle, lottery, punchboard; matching cockfight.
- Juvenile noncriminal misconduct: beyond parental control, incorrigible, runaway, truant, wayward.
- Killing domestic animal.
- Liquor: unlawful manufacture, sale, possession, consumption in public place.
- Loitering.
- Malicious mischief: painting water tower, throwing water-filled balloons, throwing rocks on highway, throwing missiles at athletic contests, throwing objects at vehicle.
- Nuisance, committing.
- Poaching.
- Possession of cigarettes by minor.
- Possession of indecent publications or pictures.
- Purchase, possessions or consumption of alcoholic beverages by minor.
- Removing property under lien.
- Removing property from public grounds.
- Robbing the orchard.
- Shooting from highway.

- Shooting on public road.
- Simple assault.
- Throwing glass or other material in road.
- Trespass to property.
- Unlawful assembly.
- Using or wearing unlawful emblem.
- Vagrancy.
- Vandalism: injuring or defacing public property or property of another, shooting out street lights.
- Violation of fireworks law.
- Violation of fish and game laws.

E–3. Misdemeanors

Offenses of comparable seriousness should be treated as non-minor misdemeanors. In doubtful cases, the following rule should be applied: if the maximum confinement under local law exceeds 4 months but not 1 year, the offense should be treated as a nonminor misdemeanor. Admitting membership in the Communist Party ("Known Communists") is also treated as a nonminor misdemeanor. The following is intended as a guide.

- Adultery.
- Assault consummated by battery.
- Bigamy.
- Breaking and entering vehicle.
- Check, worthless, making or uttering, with intent to defraud or deceive (value $100 or less).
- Contributing to delinquency of minor.
- Desecration of grave.
- Driving while drugged or intoxicated.
- Failure to stop and render aid after accident.
- Indecent exposure.
- Indecent, insulting, or obscene language communicated to another directly or by telephone.
- Leaving Dead animal.
- Looting.
- Negligent homicide.
- Petty larceny (value $100 or less); stealing hubcaps; shoplifting.
- Reckless driving (two or more offenses).
- Resisting arrest.
- Selling or leasing weapons to minors.
- Slander.
- Stolen property, knowingly receiving (value $100 or less).
- Suffrage rights, interference with.
- Unlawful carrying of firearms; carrying concealed firearms.
- Use of telephone to abuse, annoy, harass, threatens or torment another.
- Willfully discharging firearm so as to endanger life; shooting in public place.
- Wrongful appropriation of motor vehicle; joy riding; driving motor vehicle without owner's consent. This group of motor vehicle offenses, and offenses of comparable nature and seriousness but variously described (auto theft, auto larceny, and so forth), comprise the familiar case of taking or withholding a motor vehicle without authority and with intent temporarily to deprive the owner if his or her property. It does not encompass offenses where there is clear evidence that the offender intended permanently to deprive the owner of his or her motor vehicle. Offenses of the latter nature are included in grand larceny or embezzlement involving a value of over $100.
- Wrongful use or possession of marijuana.

E–4. Felonies

Offenses of comparable seriousness should be treated as felonies. In doubtful cases, the following rule will be applied: if the maximum confinement under local law exceeds 1 year, the offense should be treated as a felony.

- Aggravated assault; assault with dangerous weapon; assault intentionally inflicting great bodily harm; assault with intent to commit felony.
- Arson.
- Attempt to commit felony.
- Breaking and entering with intent to commit a felony.
- Bribery.
- Burglary.

- Carnal knowledge of a child under 16.
- Cattle rustling.
- Check, worthless, making or uttering, with intent to defraud or deceive (value over $100).
- Conspiring to commit felony.
- Criminal libel.
- Extortion.
- Forgery; knowingly uttering or passing forged instrument.
- Graft.
- Grand larceny; embezzlement (value over $100).
- Housebreaking.
- Indecent acts or liberties with child under 16.
- Indecent assault.
- Kidnapping abduction.
- Mail matter: abstracting, destroying, obstructing, opening, secreting, stealing, taking.
- Mail: depositing obscene or indecent matter.
- Maiming; disfiguring.
- Manslaughter.
- Misprision of felony.
- Murder.
- Narcotics or habit forming drugs; wrongful possessions use, sale.
- Pandering.
- Perjury; subordination of perjury.
- Public records: altering, concealing, destroying, mutilating, obliterating, removing.
- Rape.
- Riot.
- Robbery.
- Sedition; solicitation to commit sedition.
- Forcible sodomy.
- Stolen Property, possessing, selling, and so forth.

Appendix F
Management Control Evaluation Checklist

F–1. Function
Military Entrance Processing Stations.

F–2. Purpose
Assist Commanders and supervisor in identifying and accessing qualified applicants and registrants into the military services.

F–3. Instructions
Answers must be based on actual observation of operations in the Military Entrance Processing Stations and a review of supporting documents.

F–4. Test questions
a. Are applicants screened according to DODI 6130.4 and AR 40–501 and other applicable directives? (that is service unique requirements as required by USMEPCOM 40–1)

b. Are mental aptitude tests administered according to applicable guidance?

c. Are qualification tests handled to prevent test loss or compromise?

d. Were fingerprints submitted for each applicant entering the military services?

F–5. Supersession
This checklist supersedes the checklist in AR 601–270 Military Entrance Processing Stations, previously published in DA Circular 11–89–1. For assistance in responding to questions, contact the functional proponent.

F–6. Comments
Help make this a better review tool. Submit comments to the HQDA (DAPE–MPA), Washington, DC 20310–0300.

Glossary

Section I
Abbreviations

AFI
Air Force Instruction

AFJI
Air Force Joint Instruction

AFQT
Armed Forces qualification test

AR
Army regulation

ASVAB
Armed Services Vocational Aptitude Battery

CAT–ASVAB
Computerized Adaptive Testing-Armed Services Vocational Aptitude Battery

CG
commanding general

CG COMDTINST
Coast Guard Commandant Instruction

DA
Department of the Army

DEP
Delayed Entry Program

DOD
Department of Defense

DODI
Department of Defense Instruction

ENTNAC
entrance national agency check

HQDA
Headquarters, Department of the Army

IRC
Inter-Service Recruitment Committee

MCO
Marine Corps order

MEPS
military entrance processing station

MET
military entrance test

NGB
National Guard Bureau

OPM
Office of Personnel Management

OPNAVINST
Chief Naval Operations Instruction

RBJ
reevaluation believed justified

RC/OC
Recruiting Commander/Operations Conference

SDDC
Surface Deployment and Distribution Command

SF
standard form

SSN
Social Security Number

SSS
Selective Service System

TC/OC
Training Commanders/Operations Conference

UCMJ
Uniform Code of Military Justice

USMEPCOM
United States Military Entrance Processing Command

Section II
Terms

Accession
An enlistment which increases the incremental strength of the regular or RC of the military services. Personnel enlisted under the DEP are not involved in this category.

Acceptability Undetermined
A registrant whose qualification for induction is pending due to—
  a. resolution of a disqualifying moral waiver problem.
  b. medical consultation, tests or other medical determinations.
  c. lack of additional medical documentations.

Administrative acceptees
Registrants who have been found acceptable for military service following an administrative determination that they possess the required capacity to achieve the minimum qualifying ASVAB score.

Adverse juvenile adjudication
Determination by a judge or jury, in juvenile court proceedings, that the juvenile is guilty of or has committed the acts alleged in the petition or complaint, based either on the merits of the case or on the juvenile's admission of guilt in the court records.
  a. Regardless of whether a sentence was then imposed, withheld, or suspended.
  b. Regardless of subsequent proceedings in the case to delete an initial determination of guilt from court records, based on the evidence of rehabilitation or a satisfactory period of probation or supervision. Examples of subsequent proceedings in juvenile courts in the United States are: expunging, record sealing, reopening the case to change the original finding of guilty or delinquency, or the plea of guilty or admission of the truth of the allegations in the petition to not guilty and dismissal of the original petition setting aside the adjudication of delinquency. Such subsequent

proceedings recognize rehabilitation but do not alter the fact that the juvenile committed the act for which he has been adjudicated.

c. The term adverse juvenile adjudication includes adjudication as a juvenile delinquent, wayward minor, youthful offender, delinquent child, juvenile offender, and declaration of the juvenile as a ward of the court. The term does not include the adjudication as a dependent neglected, or abandoned.

Applicant
An individual applying for enlistment.

Applicant Record (USMEPCOM PCN 680–3 ADP)
This product provides the enlistment qualification, medical, DEP, and accession data of an applicant that has been entered into the Command's Reporting System.

ASVAB (Armed Services Vocational Aptitude Battery)
The basic examination used by MEPS for enlistment qualification of potential members of the military services.

Command's Reporting System
Replaces MEPCOM Integrated Resource System (MIRS).

Completed medical evaluation
A full medical examination or inspection that includes all required basic elements, including evaluation of consultations, additional tests determinations and outside medical documentations if any, and including a completed physical profile and a qualification decision.

Conscientious objectors
a. Class 1–A–O. An individual determined by the SSS to be conscientiously opposed to combatant duty but not to noncombatant duty. The Class 1–A–O registrant, if otherwise qualified, is inducted and assigned to noncombatant duty in the applicable Armed Force(s).

b. Class 1–0. An individual determined by the SSS to be conscientiously opposed to both combatant and noncombatant duty in the military services. The Class 1–0 registrant, if otherwise qualified, is ordered by the SSS to perform a period of civilian work contributing to the maintenance of the national health, safety, or interest, in lieu of induction into the applicable Armed Force(s).

Consultation
A special medical examination provided by a physician who is board-certified or board-eligible in the specialty concerned. For the purpose of providing specialty expert evaluation in a medical or surgical specialty area when such evaluation is needed to determine an applicant's medical enlistment eligibility.

Consultation evaluation
The review of a consultation by a MEPS medical doctor to establish the individual's medical acceptability or reviewed by the Service Medical Waiver Review Authority for waiver consideration.

Control desk
The desk within the MEPS that monitors and controls the evaluation or processing by directing individuals to various sections.

Conviction
The determination of guilt by a court or jury, based either on the merits of the case or on the defender's plea of guilty or nolo contendere (that is, no contest) regardless of—

a. Whether the sentence was then imposed, withheld, or suspended.

b. Subsequent proceedings in the case to delete an initial determination of guilt from court records, based on the evidence of rehabilitation or satisfactory completion of a probationary period. Example of subsequent proceedings are: pardon; expungement; reopening of the case to change the original finding of guilty, plea of guilty, or nolo contendere (that is, no contest) to not guilty and dismissal of the charge; amnesty; and setting aside the record of convictions. Such subsequent proceedings recognize rehabilitation but do not alter the fact that the offender committed the criminal act.

Courtesy shipment
The accessing and shipping of an applicant previously processed and enlisted in the DEP by a different MEPS.

Data collection

The action of recognizing needed facts, and compiling and recording them for future use.

DD Form 1966

The form used by Armed Service Recruiting Components to request applicant enlistment, and by MEPS personnel to report accession data.

DEP (Delayed Entry Program)

Any of the various service programs to enlist personnel into a special inactive Reserve group pending enlistment into active service at a projected future date. A DEP enlistee is not an accession.

Disqualified

Applicant does not meet established criteria to enlist under standards prescribed by the sponsoring service.

Eloped

Describes an SSS registrant who arrived at the MEPS as directed, but who departed the MEPS in an unauthorized manner (used in the event chap 9 is implemented).

Enlistee

An individual who has enlisted into the DEP or accessed into one of the military services.

Enlistment ASVAB

A version of the ASVAB administered in MEPS and at MET sites. The enlistment ASVAB is used solely for the examination of individuals specifically applying for enlistment. This test may be a paper and pencil version or Computerized Adaptive Testing-Armed Services Vocational Aptitude Battery version.

Enlistment Packet

A set of enlistment and/or induction-related documents provided by MEPS to various service personnel centers or agencies.

Enlistment qualification testing

The administration of the ASVAB to determine enlistment eligibility for the military services.

Examination File Folder

A personal folder or form at the MEPS that contains information on an individual who has not yet become a member of a service component.

Holdover

An individual who fails to complete enlistment qualification, medical, and/or administrative processing and is scheduled to return the next day for completion or has completed processing and is awaiting transportation back to the individual's home or initial duty station. (Requires overnight lodging.)

Inductee

An individual registered with the SSS who has been inducted into the military services (used in the event chapter 9 is implemented).

Induction

Transition from civilian to military status for a period of definite military obligation under the Military Selective Service Act.

Induction processing

Examination of SSS registrants to determine whether they meet the prescribed standards for military service; and procedures for effecting and recording the induction of qualified persons into the military services.

Major Recruiting Force

    a. Army- Army Recruiting Command.
    b. Navy - Navy Recruiting Command.
    c. Air Force- Air Force Recruiting service.
    d. Marine Corps- Marine Corps Recruiting service.
    e. National Guard - State Adjutants General.

f. Coast Guard - Recruiting Command.

Local Area Recruiting Activity
   a. Army - Recruiting Battalion.
   b. Navy - Recruiting District.
   c. Air Force - Recruiting Squadron.
   d. Marine Corps - Recruiting Station.
   e. Coast Guard- Recruiting office.

Medical examination
A full medical examination or inspection that includes all required basic elements, including the evaluation of consultations, additional tests and determinations, and outside medical documentations if any, and including a completed physical profile and qualification decision. (Same as a completed medical evaluation.)

Medical prescreening errors
Any physical evaluation disqualifications or medical examination denials which occurred because of a condition that could have been detected by the recruiting service via adequate medical prescreening.

MEPS data base listing
A report providing the MEPS with a ready reference to previously submitted files and records.

MEPS Enlistment Processing System
Actions performed by the MEPS, to include enlistment qualification testing, medical examination, administrative requirements to effect an enlistment or reenlistment of an applicant, assignments and shipment of the individual to a reception station or other initial duty station, as applicable.

Military services personnel centers
The various service's military personnel record centers.

Military entrance test (MET) site
A location outside the MEPS used for the administration of the ASVAB. Either military or contracted test administrators may administer the test at the MET Site.

Noncombatant service
A noncombatant is defined as either—
   a. Service in any unit of the military services that is unarmed at all times.
   b. Any other assignments the primary function of which does not require the use of arms in combat, provided that such other assignment is acceptable to the individual concerned and does not require the individual to bear arms or be trained in their use.

One-Day Processor
An applicant, who receives enlistment qualification testing, medical examination, is sworn in as a member of the military services (induction, accession, or DEP) all on the same day.

"Papers Only" review
Review and evaluation of medical documents or statements for the purpose of determining whether a full medical examination is justified.

Physical Inspection
An interval medical history review and limited reexamination (visual inspection), required for—
   a. Entry on AD and on ADT if more than 72 hours have elapsed from the initial examination or from a subsequent inspection.
   b. Entry into the DEP and into the Reserve and National Guard if more than 30 days has elapsed from the initial examination or from a subsequent inspection.

Prior service
   a. Army. All personnel applying for enlistment in the Regular Army and Army Reserve who have 180 days or more of continuous AD.
   b. Navy.
   (1) *Navy Veterans.* Prior-service veterans whose last tour of active duty or active duty for training was in U.S. Navy

or U.S. Navy Reserve, have been discharged or released more than 24 hours, and who completed a minimum of 12 consecutive weeks of active duty or active duty for training. Ready Mariners are also considered Navy Veterans even though they may have completed less than 12 consecutive weeks active duty or active duty for training.

(2) *Other service Veterans.* Prior-service veterans whose last tour of AD was in a branch of service other than Navy and who completed a minimum of 12 consecutive weeks of active duty or active duty for training.

c. Air Force. All personnel applying for enlistment in the Regular Air Force who have 180 days or more of continuous AD.

d. Marine Corps. All personnel who have previously served in any military services or Reserve Component thereof.

e. Coast Guard. A person who has served some valid period of creditable service in any of the U.S. military services, including Reserve Components thereof.

Processing
Any work unit accomplished for an applicant within the MEPS or MET enlistment qualification testing, medical examination, contract and associated paperwork, physical inspections and special testing.

Projection
Pertains to scheduling MEPS workload; specifically an individual initially provided by name to the MEPS for the purpose of scheduling the examination and/or processing.

Qualified
Applicant meets enlistment criteria under the standards prescribed by the sponsoring military service.

Quality assurance
Actions or procedures that insure accuracy, timeliness, and completeness.

RBJ (reevaluation believed justified)
A term applied to an individual found not qualified for military service, due to a remedial medical or non-medical condition, and whom MEPS personnel believe should be reevaluated at a later date.

Reception center or station
The various services' initial enlistee reception locations (such as Ft. Jackson, Lackland, Great Lakes, or Paris Island). (Note: Not called reception center or station by Navy, Air Force, or Marine Corps.)

Record
A submission of data into the automated reporting system concerning an individual who was examined and/or processed (see file and enlistment packet).

Refused to submit
An SSS registrant who was evaluated as qualified by the MEPS but refused to be inducted (used in the event chapter 9 is implemented).

Registrant
An individual registered with the SSS for potential induction (used in the event chap 9 is implemented).

Request for examination (USMEPCOM Form 680–3A–E)
The form used by recruiting personnel for requesting applicant evaluation or processing.

Scheduled (individuals)
Pertains to the scheduling of MEPS daily workload and is equal to the total of projections and add-ons.

Search key
The data element used to identify a record on a computerized data base. The MRS search key used during record establishment is the SSAN of the individual. The MRS search key used after record establishment is the SSAN and first four letters of the individual's last name.

Selective Service Number
A number assigned by the SSS to each registrant for identification purposes. It consists of three elements as described below:

a. The first element, reading from left to right, represents the last two digits of the year in which the registrant was born (for example, if a registrant was born in 1972, the first element would be 72). In medical and other health specialists, the first element would be 5.

b. The second element will be a sequential seven-digit number, assigned to each registrant of a year group at the time his record is entered into the Registrant Information Bank. This element will begin with 0000001 and may continue to 9999999.

c. The third element will be a single number assigned by the computer and uses a check digit to identify erroneous SSN input for updating records.

Service-required data
Information required by the various services in excess of standard DOD data (such as the data contained in block 19 of the DD Form 1966).

Social Security Number (SSN)
The number assigned to the individual by the Social Security Administration.

Shipped
Accessions and inductees released from MEPS en route to reception stations.

Special purpose test
Any test, other than the ASVAB, used to evaluate individuals for jobs requiring special knowledge or for enlistment qualification.

Stakeholders' Meeting
Provides interface between the functions of recruiting and processing and Command level.

Student ASVAB
A version of the ASVAB administered in educational institutions. The result may be used for enlistment.

Walk-in
An individual who arrived early enough for examination and/or processing, but was not scheduled by name with the MEPS prior to close of business on the preceding workday.

USMEPCOM funded consultation
A specific medical consultation individually accounted for on USMEPCOM Form 37–1–2–R–E (Itemized listing of Medical Services for Medical Examinations Public Voucher and SF 1034 (Public Voucher for Purchases and Services Other Than Personal).

Section III
Special Abbreviations and Terms
This section contains no entries.

UNCLASSIFIED

PIN 004376–000

USAPD

ELECTRONIC PUBLISHING SYSTEM
OneCol FORMATTER WIN32 Version 273

PIN: 004376–000
DATE: 09-16-11
TIME: 07:23:32
PAGES SET: 62

DATA FILE: C:\WinComp\r601-270.fil
DOCUMENT: AR 601–270

SECURITY: UNCLASSIFIED
DOC STATUS: REVISION

www.ingramcontent.com/pod-product-compliance
Lightning Source LLC
Chambersburg PA
CBHW081606170526
45166CB00009B/2844

* 9 7 8 1 4 8 4 9 8 2 0 3 7 *